A Question of Identity

The Minister for Education presents Dr Michael Tierney with a shoe-horn to enable him to get another four or five hundred students into U.C.D.
Contemporary *Dublin Opinion* cartoon, from *Forty Years of Dublin Opinion* (Dublin 1967)

A Question of Identity

*The great Trinity & UCD
merger plan of the 1960s*

Patrick O'Flynn

A. & A. Farmar

© Patrick O'Flynn 2012

All rights reserved. No part of this publication may be reproduced in any form or by any means without the prior permission of the publisher or else under the terms of a licence permitting photocopying issued by the Irish Copyright Licensing Agency or a similar reproductive rights organisation.

British Library Cataloguing in Publication Data
A CIP catalogue record for this book is available from the British Library

ISBN: 978-1-906353-31-5

First published in 2012
by
A. & A. Farmar Ltd
78 Ranelagh Village, Dublin 6, Ireland
Tel +353-1-496 3625
Email afarmar@iol.ie
Web www.aafarmar.ie

Typeset and designed by A. & A. Farmar
Printed and bound by SprintPrint

For Grainne

Acknowledgements

Most of the research for this book was carried out in the archives of Trinity and UCD. I would, therefore, wish to acknowledge the assistance of Seamus Helferty and Kate Manning of the UCD Archives (for both references and photographs) and of Bernard Meehan, the Keeper of the Manuscript Rooms at Trinity. I must also thank Malcolm Byrne for his assistance in exploring the records of the Higher Education Authority and John Foley of the National University of Ireland for his help in accessing the early minutes of the Senate of the NUI. I should acknowledge, also, the anonymous leader writers in the national newspapers for their reflection of the thinking of the Irish *bien pensants* on the issues of the day.

Thanks are due to Deirdre Raftery of UCD for her early encouragement in my exploration of this topic, to John Horgan for some helpful suggestions on government attitudes to the universities at the relevant period, to Ruth Carmody for her explorations on my behalf of the records of the Department of Education in Marlborough Street and to Ellen Gallagher for her proof-reading.

I must express my gratitude to my publishers, Anna and Tony Farmar, for their help in transforming an arid thesis into what is, I hope, an interesting book.

Finally, I should thank my many colleagues and friends in Trinity and UCD from that period in the 1960s, many of them active in the fledgling Irish Federation of University Teachers, from whom I developed an admiration, respect and love for the university and its ideals

Patrick O'Flynn
September 2012

Contents

Introduction	1
1. The early development of the Irish university system 1592–1908	5
2. The Irish university institutions 1908–60	21
3. The Commission on Higher Education	57
4. The merger	79
5. Discussion and dissension	97
6. The Lenihan plan	119
7. The end of the affair	145
Appendixes	163
Bibliography	168
Index	174

Introduction

On 18 April 1967, the Minister for Education, Donogh O'Malley, announced the intention of the Irish government to merge the two Dublin university institutions, University College, Dublin and Trinity College, Dublin. A settlement which had bedevilled British and Irish political life for a great part of the 19th century and which had emerged from the compromises of the 1908 Universities Act was, once again, to be open to change. The furore engendered by this announcement occupied academic energies and debates for the next decade. Those debates ushered in the structures which define higher education in Ireland in the 21st century. Among the institutions which saw their origins in this period were the Higher Education Authority, the National Council for Educational Awards, the University of Limerick, Dublin City University, the new secular university at Maynooth and the Institutes of Technology. What were the forces which gave rise to these changes?

It is commonplace for commentators today to describe life in Ireland in the 1950s and 60s as bleak, dull and oppressive with the role of oppressor assigned to an all-pervasive Catholic Church. It is as if Ireland was a mirror image of the German Democratic Republic with the Church replacing the Stasi as controller of the thoughts and actions of its citizenry and bending the government to its will. To someone who lived through that period, this is a grossly inadequate picture.

Economically, Ireland in the 50s was indeed a bleak place for many with emigration as the destiny of about half a million people—from an overall population of under four million—during the decade. However, the myth of a self-sufficient, isolated nation, dancing at the crossroads, was being quietly interred by the end of the decade and the economic reforms introduced by Taoiseach Seán Lemass, as he implemented the ideas in T. K. Whitaker's First Programme for Economic Expansion, were to lead to a modest expansion in employment and a curtailment of emigration in the 1960s. Indeed, the early 60s saw a substantial return to Ireland of young graduates who had been forced to emigrate on graduation at the end of the previous decade.

Politically and intellectually Ireland was far from bleak at this time. In the political sphere, the generation which had led the country from 1922 had begun to retire and a younger group whose ideas were based more on the examples of mainstream European politics than on the heroic Irish models of the 1916-1922 period were coming to the fore. A number of younger politicians who were to play an important role in bringing about change were first elected to the Dáil in this period. Donogh O'Malley and Brian Lenihan were first elected in the the 1950s while in the 1960s the names of Charlie Haughey, George Colley and then Garret FitzGerald, David Thornley and Conor Cruise O'Brien first came to political prominence. While some of these came from political families, others entered electoral politics in the belief that the times they were 'a 'changin''.

A similar change—although it arose for very different reasons—took place in religious life in Ireland. Religion still mattered greatly in Ireland in the 1960s, both in terms of the religious practice of the people but also in the intellectual life of the country. Therefore, the questionings by European theologians which blossomed with the election of Pope John XXIII, and the convening of the Second Vatican Council in 1962, began a ferment of theological and intellectual debate. The Irish daily newspapers sent some of their best young reporters to cover the working of the Council and they became media stars. Groups of young Irish intellectuals, both lay and clerical, met to debate the proper way forward for the Church and these groups were not just confined to Catholics—Protestants and people of no declared religion also participated. The 'belt of the crozier', although still to be expected, was not as feared as it had been in times past. An example of this debate was to be seen in the group known to initiates as Flannery's Harriers—an informal peripatetic group set up by Fr Austin Flannery to discuss matters philosophical, social and theological.

The art world also saw a renaissance in the 1960s. A report from a Scandinavian design group in 1961 had castigated the current state of design in Ireland. The opening of an industrial design school in the National College of Art in 1962, and the inauguration of the Kilkenny Design Workshops were responses to this perceived gap. Later in the decade there came the establishment of Project 67 as a home for young independent painters and playwrights, and the ROSC exhibition in 1967 as a showcase for international developments in painting. In literature, the effective disempowerment of the Censorship Board with a new Censorship Act in 1967 opened the way for a strengthening of Irish literary life.

A sign of the new intellectual climate in Ireland at this time was the development of the Tuairim organisation. Founded in 1954 by a mainly academic group as a discussion forum for young engaged intellectuals—it had an upper age limit of 40—it produced policy documents on such topics as university education, economic development and emigration. It operated on the optimistic assumption that when people of intelligence analysed a social or political problem and produced a solution, that solution would be taken seriously by the political establishment and might well be acted upon.

Change was not so evident in the world of education. Primary education was organised much as it had been since the settlement of 1831 with the schools under the management of local clerics of the different denominations and financed by the State. Secondary education was carried out on a binary model. A system of vocational education was managed by the local authorities under the 1930 Vocational Education Act while academic secondary education was carried out in private fee-paying schools largely owned by religious congregations or, in the case of non-Catholic schools, by clerically related groups. Higher education was monopolised by the universities which, in the case of Trinity, operated under a Charter granted by Elizabeth I in 1594 and Letters Patent of 1911. The National University of Ireland institutions, on the other hand, were governed by the terms of the University of Ireland Act of 1908.

The number of students in Irish universities was small—although the participation rate was significantly higher than in the UK. However, it was beginning to rise; the number of full-time students in University College, Dublin rose by 90 per cent between 1955/6 and 1964/5 while in Trinity there was an increase of 78 per cent over the same period. This would have been a cause of financial concern to government which took responsibility for all of the capital costs and most of the running costs of the universities.

The educational philosophy of the Department of Education was summarised by the Fine Gael Minister for Education, General Richard Mulcahy, in a reply to a parliamentary question from the opposition spokesman in 1956. He declined to philosophise about education, stating that he did not regard it as his function to do so as he saw himself as 'a kind of dungaree man, the plumber who will ... take the knock out of the pipes and will link up everything.' However, two Fianna Fáil successors to Mulcahy as Minister for Education, Dr Patrick Hillery and Donogh O'Malley, were to assume a much more positive role in the development of the Irish education system. Most notably, O'Malley's initiative in introducing free secondary education in 1966 completely altered the educational landscape at second level and created the probability of a massive increase in the numbers of students seeking entrance to the universities.

This was the background to O'Malley's speech in April 1967 proposing the merger of Trinity College and University College, Dublin.

1. The early development of the Irish university system 1592–1908

Trinity College, Dublin

The oldest university institution in Ireland, Trinity College, Dublin, was founded in 1592. Its Charter described it as *'unum Collegium matrem Universitatis'* giving it an identity as both a college and a university. Its university identity might be seen as endowing it with the capacity to develop as a multi-collegiate university in the same manner as its models in the universities of Oxford and Cambridge. However, although this dual character was the object of serious debate in later times,[1] for all practical purposes, Dublin University and Trinity College have been seen as a single entity for most of their history and are so treated in this work.

McDowell and Webb describe the background to the foundation as follows:

> ... by 1590 the royal writ ran throughout three provinces, and Dublin, the centre of military, judicial and civil administration, was well on its way to becoming a real capital. Its population comprised not only the merchants and craftsmen clustered round the port, but also soldiers, civil servants, lawyers and divines.[2]

Dublin Corporation was persuaded that it should grant to a new university the confiscated land of the priory of All Hallows. By such a foundation, the interests of both Church and State would be served while, at the same time, Dublin would benefit from the increase in trade which was expected to be brought about by the presence of a university. The Crown would improve its hold on its Irish possessions

---

1 Various schemes put forward in the 19th and early 20th centuries to provide for an extension of university education for non-Anglican students proposed that additional colleges be incorporated into Dublin University. None of these schemes came to fruition.

2 McDowell, R. B. and D. A. Webb (1982). *Trinity College Dublin, 1592–1952: An academic history.* Cambridge, Cambridge University Press.

*Chancellor Éamon de Valera listens to Michael Tierney at an NUI meeting in the Senate Room of the NUI offices in Merrion Square. Note the prominent presence of senior Catholic clergy (*Irish Press*).*

by halting the practice whereby young men from both the Gaelic and Anglo-Norman families sought their education in France and Spain; the Reformed Church would have a place wherein its clergy could be educated and trained. And so, Queen Elizabeth I granted a charter to the new *Collegium sanctae et Individuae Trinitatis juxta Dublin a Serenissima Regina Elizabetha fundatum*.

Maynooth

In its early years, a certain number of the children of Catholic aristocratic families attended at Trinity College. In 1637, however, new statutes were introduced which made it impossible for Catholics to register as students without renouncing their religious affiliation.[3] These restrictions were eased by the Catholic Relief Act of 1793 but restrictions on the holding of professorships, fellowships and scholarships by non-Anglicans remained until the passing of Fawcett's Act in 1873. As a result, Catholic students, to a large extent, sought their university education in continental Europe, mainly in France. This was particularly the case for those studying for the Catholic priesthood.

P. J. Corish, in his history of Maynooth, gives an account of the development of Catholic seminaries in Europe in the years after the Council of Trent. He notes that by the end of the 18th century, nearly 500 seminary places for Irish clerical students had been provided in major seminaries in Paris, Nantes, Douai, Louvain, Salamanca, Rome and elsewhere.[4]

Although this method of provision of clergy for the Catholic Church in Ireland was technically illegal under the Penal Laws[5] which were still in force, the Irish government turned a blind eye to the practice.

---

3 Coolahan, J. (1981). *Irish Education—History and Structure*. Dublin, Institute of Public Administration.

4 Corish, P. J. (1995). *Maynooth College 1795–1995*. Dublin, Gill & Macmillan, pp. 1–6. Coolahan (op. cit.) gives a figure of 478 for the number of Irish students attending foreign institutions in the year of the French Revolution, 1789. It is not specified whether this figure includes clerical students. Corish cites figures given to parliament in 1808 by the secretary of the trustees of Maynooth College.

5 The Penal Laws consisted of a series of enactments brought in after the victory of the Williamite cause in 1691 with the intention of consolidating the Protestant hegemony in Ireland. By 1745 they were mostly dead letters though they persisted in one form or another until Catholic emancipation was conceded by the Westminster government in 1829.

However, with the growth of radical ideologies in France, even in the seminaries, in the later years of the 18th century, both the government and the Church authorities became alarmed at the prospect of the dissemination of dangerous democratic ideals in Ireland by returned clerics. It was in both their interests, therefore, to work towards the provision of a seminary education for Irish Catholic clerics at home.

What eventually emerged was the 1795 legislation entitled 'An Act for the better education of persons professing the Popish or Roman Catholic Religion', which established a college to be named the Royal College of St Patrick, Maynooth. The college was not to be a chartered institution and had no endowment. However, it was to be supported by an annual grant from parliament. It was to be governed by a board of trustees which, although it contained laymen, was dominated by members of the Catholic hierarchy. The Act allowed for the education of non-clerical students at Maynooth and Catholic lay students did attend there in its early years. However, a Visitation of the college in 1801 reported to the government that 'as this was likely to prejudice the monopoly enjoyed then by Trinity College ... the lay college should be closed.'[6] Admission of lay students to Maynooth finally ceased in 1817 and was not formally allowed again until 1966.

As a non-chartered body, Maynooth could not grant degrees to its graduates. However, in 1896, the authority to confer degrees in theology, philosophy and canon law was granted by Rome to St Patrick's College and the college assumed the status of a pontifical university.[7] Degrees for studies in the other areas of the college subsequently became available from the Royal University of Ireland.

The 'godless colleges'

With the decision of the trustees to terminate the attendance of non-clerical students at Maynooth and the continued prohibition on the admission of non-Anglican students to Trinity College, there was still no provision for the education of lay Catholic or, indeed of non-Anglican Protestant, students in Ireland. The Catholic hierarchy

---

6 Corcoran, T., (Ed.) (1932). *Ollsgoil na hÉireann: The National University Handbook 1908–1932*. Dublin, Sign of the Three Candles.

7 A pontifical university is an institution licensed by the Vatican to conduct studies and grant degrees in Church-related subjects.

believed that education for Catholics, at all levels, must be under their control. However, a new generation of Catholic lay people was emerging which did not give unequivocal support to their bishops in this regard.

Coolahan[8] and O'Flynn[9] give comprehensive accounts of the discussions and negotiations which went on during this period in an attempt to secure higher education for the emerging Catholic middle class and for the Presbyterians of Ulster. It emerged clearly from those discussions that universities governed by the Catholic hierarchy would never be countenanced by a Westminster government. British politicians, therefore, came to believe that a new model of higher education institution, distinct from the clerically governed institutions at Oxbridge and in Dublin University, was needed. This came with the foundation of London University and its colleges in England in the 1820s and 1830s. These institutions, which were vigorously opposed by different elements in British society and denounced widely as 'godless colleges', were governed by lay trustees and admitted students of any religion and of none. Moreover, they were non-residential and allowed external students to sit their examinations and take their degrees. The use of this model as a solution to the problem of educating lay Catholics in Ireland was to meet a similar denunciation.

The Queen's University in Ireland

In 1845 Sir Robert Peel introduced a Bill which had the effect of establishing three non-denominational colleges in Ireland; these were to become the Queen's Colleges in Cork, Galway and Belfast.[10] The colleges were to be secular in their government and their teaching, and all appointments, both to the administrative offices and to the professoriate, were to be made by the Crown. They were to be non-residential but there was no prohibition on the establishment of privately funded residences for students. Similarly, there was no prohibition on the private funding of religious teaching other than that

---

8 Coolahan, op. cit.

9 O'Flynn, G. (1973). 'The Dublin Episcopate and the Higher Education of Roman Catholics in Ireland 1793–1908'. Unpublished M.Ed. thesis, Trinity College Dublin.

10 Murphy, J. A. (1995). *The College—A History of Queen's/University College Cork*. Cork, Cork University Press.

Table 1.1 Student numbers in the Queen's Colleges 1849–79

Annual average	Queen's, Belfast	Queen's, Cork	Queen's, Galway	Totals
1849–59	189	147	85	421
1859–69	368	234	147	749
1869–79	400	253	153	806

Source: Moody and Beckett (1959) p. 140

attendance at such teaching would not be required of any student.

The colleges opened for teaching in 1849 and the Queen's University was established by charter in 1850 with sole power of examining for its degrees. The university was to have its seat in Dublin although it never acquired premises in the city; it met in Dublin Castle and held its examinations there. It was to be governed by a chancellor, appointed for life by the Crown; a senate consisting of the presidents of the three Queen's Colleges and 17 other members appointed for life by the Crown and representing all the principal departments of learning; and by a vice-chancellor elected annually by the senate from its own members. The chancellor and the senate were to make regulations for all courses of study and for degree examinations.[11]

Reaction among the various groupings in Ireland to the establishment of the Queen's Colleges was divided. Coolahan summarises the position as follows:

> Daniel O'Connell, the prestigious leader of the Repeal Association, denounced the proposed colleges as 'the godless colleges'... and said that nothing but Catholic colleges would satisfy Catholic demands. Thomas Davis, leader of the Young Ireland Group, praised the measure, seeing it as an opportunity for promoting understanding and fellowship among young Irish people of different religious beliefs. The Catholic hierarchy was divided: a minority led by Dr Murray of Dublin and Dr Crolly of Armagh looked with some favour on the colleges; the majority, led by Dr MacHale of Tuam, condemned them.[12]

The wavering of some of the hierarchy on the issue was ended by the strong direction of the newly appointed Archbishop of Armagh, Dr Paul Cullen, at the Synod of Thurles in 1850. The synod condemned

---

[11] Moody, T. W. and J. C. Beckett (1959) *Queen's Belfast: 1845–1949*. Belfast, Faber & Faber.

[12] Coolahan, op. cit.

the new colleges as unacceptable for the higher education of Catholics and issued a strong statement on the dangers of inter-denominational education. Despite this denunciation from the Catholic hierarchy, experience over the next three decades showed that a considerable number of Catholic students ignored it.

Moody and Beckett (Tables 1.1 opposite) note the figures for the attendance of students at the Queen's Colleges from 1849 to 1879.

For comparison, they note that, over the same period, the number of students on the books in Trinity College ranged between 1,000 and 1,600. They also give the religious denomination of the students at Queen's College, Belfast over the same period.

Table 1.2 Religious denomination of students in Queen's College, Belfast 1849–79

	1849–59 %	1859–69 %	1869–79 %
Presbyterians	70	66	59
Church of Ireland	19	15	20
Methodists	2	4	6
Other Protestants	2	9	11
Roman Catholics	7	5	4

Source: Moody and Beckett (1959) p. 194

Murphy[13] notes that there were 146 Catholic students out of a total of 280 students, or 52 per cent, in attendance in Queen's College, Cork in the 1879–80 session.

The Catholic University

Following the failure of the Catholic hierarchy to have any significant influence on the development of the Queen's University system, the bishops saw it as imperative to develop a new university which was owned and controlled by them. Cardinal Cullen, now Archbishop of Dublin, assumed the leading role in this development. O'Flynn[14] and McCartney[15] give detailed accounts of the discussions within the hierarchy and with others, including leading English Catholics, over the form which this development might take. Overcoming the claims of sites such as Thurles or Wales, the Catholic University was established

---

13 Op. cit.
14 Op. cit.
15 McCartney, D. (1999). *UCD: A National Idea—The History of University College, Dublin*. Dublin, Gill & Macmillan, pp. 1–4.

in Dublin in buildings on St Stephen's Green under the rectorship of John Henry Newman in 1854.[16]

The new institution was governed directly by the Catholic bishops although a certain degree of autonomy was given to Newman as Rector. It had four faculties—Arts, Theology, Medicine and Law—but no charter and, therefore, no state-recognised degree-awarding powers. In its early years, debate continued over the precise role it should seek to play, between those who saw it as a great international university for English-speaking Catholics and those whose more modest vision was for a substantial university institution for the growing Irish Catholic middle class. The model of Louvain, which had been re-established as the Catholic University of Louvain in 1835, was held up as an example to follow.

The history of the Catholic University for its first 30 years did not reflect the hopes of its founders. It was funded primarily by annual collections made in each Catholic parish and the amounts raised, varying from £4,000 to £9,600, rarely met its running costs. Newman resigned as Rector in 1858 to be succeeded by a succession of Irish clerics of whom his immediate successor, Monsignor Bartholomew Woodlock,[17] had the most substantial role in its development. Its student numbers were never very great. McCartney reports that, excluding the medical school, in its first 25 years the annual student intake averaged only about 20.

The exclusion of medical students from this analysis arises from the fact that the one exception to the relative failure of the Catholic University was its medical school. As McCartney writes, 'the Catholic University Medical School prospered largely because it adapted its courses to those of the chartered licensing bodies, from which it formally sought recognition, and students who passed the examinations were granted a licence to practise, mainly through the Royal College of Surgeons in Ireland.'[18] Based in Cecilia Street in Dublin, it became the largest medical school in Ireland and, on the incorporation of

---

16 O'Flynn, op. cit., p. 79, notes that at one stage, Cullen favoured Thurles as a site, arguing that 'the town was poor and wretched and offered no temptations to youth.'

17 Monsignor Woodlock served as Rector from 1860 to 1879. He was subsequently Bishop of Ardagh and Clonmacnoise.

18 McCartney, op. cit.

University College, Dublin into the National University of Ireland in 1908, it became the medical faculty of the new university college.

The Catholic University suffered from many disadvantages. Most significantly, it had no endowment or annual government grant and it lacked a charter which would allow it to award recognised degrees. The hierarchy continued to lobby the government in the 1860s and 70s to overcome these defects and various schemes were put forward at different times. The strength of non-conformist opinion in British political life was such that it was always unlikely that a British government—Liberal or Conservative—would grant money towards an institution governed directly by the Catholic Church. Nonetheless, proposals which might have provided for degree-granting powers were considered. A plan to incorporate the Catholic University as an unendowed college of the Queen's University was defeated by Queen's graduates. Another plan to have the Catholic University incorporated as a college within Dublin University, with equal status to Trinity College, was put forward by the bishops but was rejected by the government. Finally, in 1873 Gladstone's first Liberal government[19] brought forward a Bill which would have abolished the Queen's University and reconstituted Dublin University to incorporate all the colleges in Ireland—the Queen's Colleges and the Catholic University along with Trinity College—although without an endowment for the Catholic University. This Bill was defeated in parliament leading to the resignation of Gladstone's government. It was a Conservative government led by Benjamin Disraeli which abolished the Queen's University in 1889 and established the Royal University.

The Royal University

The establishment of the Royal University and the abolition of the Queen's University avoided the main stumbling block for Gladstone's failed attempt—any suggestion that the position of Trinity College would be disturbed. It differed from its predecessor in that, instead of having the strong centralising structures of the Queen's University, it was an examining and not a teaching body, which accepted as candidates for its examinations and degrees students from any college

---

19 Gladstone's first ministry was in office from 1868 to 1874. Gladstone was succeeded by Benjamin Disraeli who was in office as Prime Minister until 1880.

or from none. It also was noteworthy in that, for the first time in Ireland, women were accepted equally with men as candidates for its examinations and degrees.

The establishment of the Royal University gave the Queen's Colleges an independence which they did not particularly cherish. An immediate outcome of the change was that their student numbers began to fall. Coolahan gives figures for this fall by noting that, whereas in 1881–2, the numbers in Queen's, Belfast, Cork and Galway were 567, 402 and 201 respectively, by 1901 these numbers were reduced to 349, 190 and 93.[20] In the same year, 1901, only 500 of the 1,779 successful candidates at the Royal University examinations came from the Queen's Colleges although these tended to dominate the university's exhibition and scholarship results sheets. A large number of the candidates came from Catholic secondary schools such as Blackrock College, run by the Holy Ghost congregation, and the Jesuit schools in Tullabeg and Dublin which had set up facilities to educate students for the Royal University examinations. The Protestant secondary schools, Alexandra College in Dublin and Victoria College in Belfast, were also quick to seize the opportunity to get university qualification for women and they were followed in this endeavour by Catholic schools of the Dominican and Loreto orders.[21]

One important aspect of the Royal University's operations was that it was able to offer 32 fellowships to staff members in the colleges which educated students for its examinations. These fellowships, valued at £400 per annum, provided a significant, if indirect, method of funding the development of the Catholic University.

The Royal College of Science in Ireland

One further, substantial, development in this period was the establishment of the Royal College of Science in 1867. This was an evolutionary development from the work of Robert Kane[22] in developing

---

20 Coolahan, op. cit.

21 Raftery, D. and S. M. Parkes (2007). *Female education in Ireland 1700–1900: Minerva or Madonna.* Dublin, Irish Academic Press, pp 110–14.

22 Sir Robert Kane (1809–90) was one of the most respected Irish scientists of the 19th century. Celebrated for his seminal work *The Industrial Resources of Ireland* published in 1844, he was at various times, the President of Queen's College, Cork, Vice-Chancellor of the Royal University, Head of the Royal College of Science in

the Museum of Economic Geology and its collaboration with the Royal Dublin Society in offering courses in science and technology. The Royal College of Science was established with an annual parliamentary grant and, whereas it did not have degree-granting authority, its awards of associateship of the college (ARCSI), given to those who successfully completed its professional courses, were regarded as equivalent to degrees by the professional bodies of engineers and scientists.

The Royal College of Science was a success and it attracted significant numbers of students. For much of its history, however, a majority of the students of the college were British rather than Irish and its impact on the broader Irish higher education system was not substantial. The college was finally absorbed into University College, Dublin in 1926. One may note as evidence for the regard in which science and technology were held in the 19th century in Ireland that there appears to have been no significant objection by religious or political figures to the development of this particular secular 'godless' college.

The fate of the Catholic University

The establishment of the Royal University of Ireland in 1879 did not, as the government might have hoped, provide a final answer to the Irish university question but in its development, the need for an answer became clearer. As noted above, the Queen's Colleges did not prosper under the new regime, demonstrating that Catholic acceptance of that particular approach to the solution of the university problem was, at best, lukewarm. On the other hand, the proliferation of institutions preparing students for the examinations of the Royal University illustrated the growing demand of Catholic Ireland for university education.

The position of the Catholic University was anomalous. While, on the one hand, a form of Catholic higher education was flourishing in institutions managed by the Holy Ghost Fathers, and by the Jesuit order and in the Catholic seminaries at Maynooth and elsewhere, student enrolment languished in the university in St Stephen's Green. The Jesuits were particularly successful in establishing thriving institutions, at Tullabeg in Carlow and later, at St Ignatius in Temple

Ireland and President of the Royal Irish Academy.

Street in Dublin, whose students consistently outshone their counterparts from St Stephen's Green in the examinations of the Royal University.

A decision was taken by the Catholic hierarchy in 1879 that the Catholic University should become a federal institution with a number of constituent colleges. Henceforth, the Catholic University was to consist of St Patrick's College, Maynooth; University College, St Stephen's Green; St Patrick's, Carlow; the French College, Blackrock;[23] Holy Cross, Clonliffe; St Kieran's College, Kilkenny; Mount Carmel, Terenure; the Medical School, Cecilia Street and St Ignatius' College, Temple Street.[24]

The new federal Catholic University had an insignificant history, being always less than the sum of its parts. Having neither teaching nor examining functions, its influence on its constituent colleges was minimal. It faded away in time and its gradual departure was scarcely noticed. It survived only in the persons of its trustees—the four Catholic archbishops.[25]

The continuing success of the Jesuits in their colleges led to moves within the hierarchy to invite them to take over the management of University College in St Stephen's Green. Despite the reservations of some of the bishops, these moves came to fruition when the college was handed over to the Jesuits in October 1883 and William Delaney SJ[26] assumed the presidency of the college, to be known henceforth as University College, Dublin (UCD).

UCD flourished under the management of Delaney and the Jesuits—particularly in its later years—so that in 1907, in a debate in parliament, Tom Kettle MP was able to state that 'in every year

23 The Holy Ghost Fathers were originally referred to as the French Fathers.
24 The inclusion of the Jesuit College in Temple Street may be seen as an attempt by the Catholic hierarchy to control the work of the Jesuits who were, some of the bishops feared, engaged in an aggressive plan to dominate higher education for Catholics in Ireland.
25 The trustees remained as the owners of the buildings of the Catholic University, numbers 83–86, St Stephen's Green; the freehold of numbers 85 and 86 was finally acquired from them by University College, Dublin in 1986.
26 William Delaney (1835–1924) was a prominent Jesuit educator. He was President of University College, Dublin during most of the period between its transition from being the Catholic University to its incorporation as a constituent college of the new National University of Ireland in 1908.

and every examination for at least the last five years . . . the single unendowed University [college] had secured more first-class honours and distinctions of every kind than the three Queen's Colleges put together'.²⁷

The National University of Ireland

The stage was now set for the final battle in the struggle for the provision of university education for Catholics in Ireland. The Irish university question was to become, along with the fight for home rule and a solution to the land problem, a dominant political issue in Anglo-Irish relations for the next quarter of a century.

The Royal University of Ireland had brought about significant change in the fortunes of the main institutions outside Trinity College. One phenomenon to which it contributed was the accelerated growth of an educated Catholic middle class, whose political leaders in the Irish Parliamentary Party in Westminster were to play an important role in future developments. The Catholic hierarchy remained the main protagonist on the Catholic side of the issue although, after the death of Cardinal Cullen in 1878, it was less assured in its stance and by the end of the century was divided into different camps led, unofficially, by Archbishop Walsh of Dublin and Bishop O'Dwyer of Limerick.²⁸ By this time, also, the unequivocal demand of the hierarchy that any university intended for Catholics should be governed by it had been diluted.

The other main protagonist in this debate was Dublin University and its one college, Trinity College, Dublin. Although the remaining legal restrictions on the attendance of Catholics at Trinity had been removed in 1873, Trinity was still thought of, by Protestants and Catholics alike, as a pillar of the Protestant, unionist ascendancy in

27 McCartney, op. cit. p. 22. Tom Kettle (1880–1916) was a nationalist MP at Westminster and Professor of National Economics at University College Dublin. He enlisted in the British Army during the Great War and was killed at the Battle of the Somme in 1916.

28 Paseta, Senia. (2000). 'The Catholic Hierarchy and the Irish University Question, 1880–1908'. History Vol. 85, Issue 278, pp. 268–85. Paseta gives a comprehensive account of this period and of the conflicts between O'Dwyer and Walsh. Other historians (O'Flynn, op. cit.; McCartney, op. cit.) give a more sympathetic view of Walsh than that given by Paseta. Edward O'Dwyer, one of the most outspoken members of the Irish hierarchy, was Bishop of the Limerick diocese from 1886 to 1917.

Ireland.[29] In its existing structures, therefore, it was seen by mainstream Catholic opinion as an unacceptable university for Catholic students. In fact, in 1875 the Catholic hierarchy had imposed a formal ban on the attendance of Catholics at Trinity.[30] Trinity accepted this role happily and fought strongly to repel any encroachments on to its hallowed, and generously endowed, lawns.

Governments, both Liberal and Conservative, accepted that a new solution was required. The Irish Party at Westminster, particularly after the Parnellite split had been healed under the leadership of John Dillon and John Redmond, pursued the issue vigorously. Archbishop Walsh played a strong leadership role in keeping the question at the forefront of debate and in keeping the political leaders in touch with Catholic concerns.

A Conservative government under Lord Salisbury, and later under Arthur Balfour, in 1901, established a Royal Commission on University Education in Ireland—known as the Robertson Commission after its chairman—to come up with a solution. Its terms of reference precluded any discussion of the place of Trinity College. When it reported in 1903, its primary conclusion, that the Royal University should become a federal teaching and examining institution with four colleges—the three Queen's Colleges and a new Catholic college—received little welcome or support from any of the significant parties in the debate.

When the Liberal party was returned to office under Campbell-Bannerman in 1905, a new Royal Commission on Trinity College, Dublin was established; this commission was known as the Fry Commission after its chairman, Sir Edward Fry. It was charged with advising on the steps that might be taken to increase the usefulness to the country of Trinity College and the University of Dublin. The conclusions of the Fry Commission (published in 1907) were, in summary, that the University of Dublin should become a national federal university, that a new college acceptable to Catholics should be established in Dublin, that the new college, along with Trinity and the Queen's Colleges in Cork and Belfast, should be constituent colleges

---

29 By this time, the Queen's College in Belfast was, *de facto*, as much a Presbyterian institution as Trinity was, *de jure*, a Church of Ireland one.

30 The ban, first imposed in 1875, was continued in various formulations until finally removed in 1970.

of the new federal university and that St Patrick's, Maynooth, Queen's College, Galway and Magee College[31] should become affiliated colleges of the university.

The Catholic hierarchy were, in general, pleased with these recommendations. However, a vigorous campaign by Trinity and its friends in England, allied to stern opposition from Queen's, Belfast, ensured that they would not be brought forward as legislative proposals. It was left to Augustine Birrell, appointed Chief Secretary for Ireland in 1907, to come up with a solution which was acceptable to Irish opinion and which was politically feasible.

In entering into negotiations on the form which legislation might take, Birrell had the benefit of observing the reactions to the reports of the Robertson and the Fry Commissions and was determined to avoid their mistakes. His chief partner in these negotiations was Archbishop Walsh through whom he hoped to avoid condemnation by the Catholic hierarchy.[32] Whereas Walsh was not supported enthusiastically by all his fellow bishops, his position of authority on the university question was, however grudgingly, accepted by them. Walsh also had strong links with the leaders of the Irish Parliamentary Party.

Birrell finally introduced the Irish Universities Bill in parliament in March 1908 with the assurance of support from the Conservative opposition. It passed through all stages with little antagonism and was enacted into law in August 1908. The main provisions of the Irish Universities Act were:

- The Royal University was abolished.
- The Queen's College in Belfast was established as the Queen's University, Belfast.
- A new college was established in Dublin; although not specified in the Act, this was to be the new identity of the Jesuit

---

31 Magee was a college established in Londonderry in 1865 to provide education and training for Presbyterian clergymen.

32 The most comprehensive treatment of these negotiations is given by O'Flynn (op. cit.). T. J. Morrissey in *Towards a National University: William Delaney (1835–1924)*. Dublin, 1983, Wolfhound Press., J. Coolahan in Chapter 1 of T. Dunne, (Ed.) *The National University of Ireland 1908–2008*. Dublin, 2008, University College Dublin Press, p. 40, Paseta (op. cit.), and McCartney (op. cit.) have also given detailed accounts.

University College.[33]
- A new university was established in Dublin called the National University of Ireland. The Queen's Colleges in Cork and Galway, along with the new University College in Dublin were to be the constituent colleges of the new university.
- The new universities were given the power to have recognised colleges whose students would have all the benefits of matriculated students in the constituent colleges.
- There was no provision for clerical involvement in the management of the university or its constituent colleges. However, the criteria set down for the membership of the governing bodies of the new institutions ensured that they would be acceptable to the majority Catholic, population.
- There was no reference to Trinity College or to Dublin University in the legislation.

The mechanism whereby the new universities could have recognised colleges, allowed for the rapid *de facto* incorporation of St Patrick's College, Maynooth into the new system; any proposal which might have been made to incorporate it as a constituent college would almost certainly have led to the defeat of the Bill in parliament.[34]

The 1908 Act proved to be an enduring settlement of the Irish university question. The arrangements established in the Act survived, essentially unchanged, for the next 90 years.

---

33 The names of the new institutions were not specified in the Act; they were to be specified in the Charters granted to them.

34 Magee College became a recognised college of the new Queen's University in Belfast.

2. The Irish university institutions 1908–60

The National University of Ireland

The 1908 settlement made provision for the establishment of two new universities—the National University of Ireland (NUI) based in Dublin and the Queen's University in Belfast. Queen's developed more or less independently and, after the establishment of the Irish Free State in 1922, it took its place in the British university system. The NUI was to become the main channel for the provision of university education in Ireland for most of the next century.

To ensure the acceptance of the new National University by the Catholic and nationalist population, the Act established the Dublin Commission with a brief to write the first statutes for the university and its colleges and to apportion faculties and staff between them. The membership of this body, under the chairmanship of Chief Justice Baron Palles[1] was designed to ensure its acceptability.[2] Similarly, the first Senate of the university, whose membership was specified in the Charter granted under the Act, was sufficiently representative of the various interests whose approval was important in gaining the necessary public support. The Senate at its first meeting unanimously elected Archbishop Walsh as its Chancellor.[3]

In a further move which established its Catholic credentials, the university quickly accepted those elements of the teaching programme

---

1 Chief Baron Palles (1831–1920) was a Catholic graduate of Trinity and a distinguished jurist who held the office of Lord Chief Baron of Her Majesty's Court of the Exchequer in Ireland.

2 McCartney, op. cit., pp. 68–76, discusses Birrell's strategy to ensure acceptance of the new body. There were some who were not convinced by him, including Bishop O'Dwyer of Limerick who had warned that the university about to be established in Dublin had been 'structured by a non-conformist Chief Secretary in consultation with the Free Churches who had palmed off on an unsuspecting Irish public, a rank un-denominational institution full of dangers' (O'Flynn, op. cit., p. 334).

3 Walsh remained as Chancellor until his death in 1921. He was followed in this office by Éamon de Valera who served for more than 50 years until 1975.

of St Patrick's College, Maynooth which were concerned with lay studies, as a recognised college under the terms of the Act. It then co-opted the President of Maynooth as a member of the Senate and subsequently named him as a pro-vice chancellor, with similar status to the presidents of the constituent colleges. This development had been envisaged by Birrell in drafting the Act and had been anticipated by the hierarchy. From then on, the university, insofar as it was allowed under the Act, treated Maynooth as of equal standing with the constituent colleges.[4] All other applications for recognised college status were rejected by the NUI for the next 50 years.

Powers of the NUI

Both the earlier Queen's University and its successor, the Royal University, had governing bodies which, apart from a small number of *ex officio* appointments, were nominated exclusively by the Crown. The NUI, however, was structured so that, apart from four members nominated by the Crown, the Senate was controlled by academics from the constituent colleges. Similarly, the governing authorities of the constituent colleges, as specified in their Charters, were dominated by academic members of those colleges. This form of academic government gave the new university institutions the essential elements to guard against state encroachment on their autonomy. In practice, university autonomy has been unchallenged until modern times.

The NUI Charter gave the university the powers to control, in a general way, the academic activities of the constituent colleges, to establish matriculation standards and to make all the most significant appointments, including to the presidency, in the colleges. The complex mechanisms through which university approval was required for the establishment of new courses and curricula in the colleges did not inhibit developments, and all of the colleges saw substantial additions to their academic offerings in the early years.

In later years, tensions occasionally arose when proposals for academic development from one college might be seen to have been blocked by an alliance of the other two colleges' representatives on the

---

4 Corcoran, for example, in his celebratory *National University Handbook* (op. cit.) published on the 25th anniversary of the foundation of the NUI, does not distinguish in any significant way between the recognised and the constituent colleges.

Senate. In still later times, after the period under discussion in this chapter, it appears that there was an unspoken agreement among the colleges that they would not interfere in each other's affairs.

The other mechanism through which the university exercised academic control over the colleges was its power to appoint external examiners to them. This power was used, effectively, to ensure that academic standards in the new colleges were equivalent to those in the British university system.

One academic matter which led to considerable heated debate in the first year of the university's existence was the demand made by the Gaelic League that the Irish language should be a compulsory subject for matriculation in the university. This move was opposed by the Catholic hierarchy who feared that it might induce students to register in Trinity, where such a requirement did not exist. At a meeting of the Senate in June 1909, Douglas Hyde,[5] President of the Gaelic League and a member of the Senate, proposed the resolution that Irish should be a compulsory subject for matriculation. Having been referred to the board of studies and to the three constituent colleges, the proposal was finally carried by 21 votes to 12 at a meeting of the Senate on 23 June 1910. This vote was influenced perhaps as much by declarations from a number of county councils that scholarships to the NUI would not be funded by them if the resolution was defeated, as by the cultural arguments on the issue. Gearóid Ó Tuathaigh has commented that this 'was probably the only occasion in recent Irish history on which a significant volume of public opinion ensured that language trumped religion as the key marker of Irish cultural identity within the nationalist community in Ireland.'[6] The effect of 'compulsory Irish' on the competition for students among Irish university institutions has remained a significant issue for the NUI ever since, as Trinity has always rejected any proposal that it should adopt a similar approach to the national language.

---

5 Douglas Hyde (1860–1949) was also Professor of Modern Irish at UCD and first President of Ireland from 1938 to 1945.

6 'The Position of the Irish Language' in Dunne (Ed.) op. cit., p. 40.

A QUESTION OF IDENTITY

Appointments

The Charter of the NUI set down the duty of the university to appoint and remove presidents, professors and lecturers of the constituent colleges, in accordance with the Act and with the Charters of the colleges. The procedures established were intended to ensure that local loyalties would not over-ride academic considerations in making appointments. For the appointment of professors and lecturers, for example, the governing body of the college was required to seek the prior advice of the academic council. In turn, the academic councils sought the advice of those college faculties in which the persons appointed would be members. The results of these consultations were then forwarded to the Senate. In practice, therefore, the appointment of a professor or lecturer involved the votes of at least four separate bodies with the decisive vote being that of the Senate. To inform the various electorates, candidates in UCD, for example, were required to submit 150 bound copies of their applications.

The procedure of appointing assessment boards to make an expert assessment of the merits of the candidates was not instituted until the 1960s so that canvassing of the various electorates became an essential feature of the process. In a university whose genesis had been the outcome of an intense political debate over many years, it was not surprising that politics, both academic and national, sometimes intruded into the arena.[7] Despite occasional disputes, it can be said nevertheless that the appointment system of the NUI operated as was intended. The role of the Senate as an inter-institutional body ensured that local loyalties did not prevail over academic merit in making appointments to the colleges.

The NUI survived unchanged from 1908 to 1997. There were resentments at times over the restrictions imposed by the federal system. At the time of its foundation, there was considerable pressure from UCC to gain independence as a University of Munster. By the 1950s,

---

7 An early indication of the public interest in university appointments appears in the minutes of the Senate for 27 October 1911 where it is recorded that the Senate had before it 'a letter from the Town Clerk of Dublin enclosing a copy of a resolution of the Municipal Council of the City of Dublin in reference to the appointment to the Lectureship in Spanish and Italian.'

UCD felt that it had outgrown the university and that it should be independent. UCG, as the smallest of the colleges, consistently valued the federal link. Despite these differences, when the opportunity for amending university legislation finally came 90 years after its foundation, the authorities in the colleges welcomed a solution which, although it reduced the competence of the university in many areas, retained the National University of Ireland.

University College, Dublin 1908–60

In 1908, University College, Dublin was incorporated into the NUI, under the same name. Its first President was Denis Coffey,[8] previously the head of the Catholic University Medical School on Cecilia Street. Its premises were, initially, the university buildings at 85 and 86 St Stephen's Green and its academic staff and students were, largely, those who transferred from the 'old' UCD.

Governing structures

Like the other constituent colleges of the NUI, the charter of UCD established what was, in the context of the British university system of which it was then a part, a modern governing structure. The highest authority was a relatively large governing body which was composed of an amalgam of academic staff, Crown appointees, graduates and local authority representatives. Whereas the structure provided for a non-academic majority on the Governing Body, in practice, the selections by co-option and by the Senate and, in later times by the graduates, ensured that there was normally a clear majority of academic members. The large number of local authority representatives—10 out of a total of 34—was considered appropriate at the time in that, in the absence of a native government, the local authorities provided the most fully democratic representatives of the Irish people. It was also hoped that the local authorities would be a significant source of funding, through scholarships and otherwise, for the new college.

It may be noted, also, that the local authority representatives were selected by a national body—the General Council of County Councils—rather than by individual authorities in the Dublin hinterland. By contrast, for the colleges in Cork and Galway, local authority

---

8 Denis J. Coffey (1865–1945) served as President until 1940.

representatives were selected by the authorities in the surrounding counties. This can be seen as an indication that UCD was planned to have a national, as opposed to a purely local character. In popular usage in later years, UCD was referred to commonly as 'National'; this practice continued, certainly into the 1940s, and was a source of irritation to members of UCC and UCG who were unwilling to cede this distinction to their more junior partner in Dublin.

The academic staff members of the college were defined as professors, lecturers and assistants; professors and lecturers[9] were appointed by the Senate of the NUI while assistants were appointed by the Governing Body of the college. The Academic Council, which was the highest academic authority in the college, had as members the professors of the college. The charter further created eight faculties having as members the professors and lecturers in the particular subject areas.[10] The concept of a subject department was not defined in the Charter; it evolved over the years but was never, in fact, formally defined by statute.

Religion

Section 3 of the Irish Universities Act, 1908 specified that no religious tests could be imposed by the university. Moreover, it was required of every professor upon entering into office that he should sign a declaration promising the respectful treatment of the religious opinions of his students. How were these restrictions to fit with the status of the college as the fruit of a lengthy 'struggle with fortune'[11] to provide university education for Catholics? This dilemma was more apparent than real. The prevailing Catholic ethos in Ireland in 1908 and, even

---

9 Arising from the fact that their appointment required the creation of a statute, lecturers came to be known in UCD as 'statutory lecturers'. This distinction became particularly significant when, towards the end of the period under review in this chapter, UCD created new positions of assistant lecturer and college lecturer.

10 These faculties were: Arts, Philosophy and Sociology, Celtic Studies, Science (including Technology and Agriculture), Law, Medicine, Engineering and Architecture, and Commerce. In later years, the number of faculties increased to ten with the establishment of Faculties of General Agriculture and Veterinary Medicine.

11 A phrase from Newman's 'Idea of a University' used as the title of a book by President Michael Tierney on the history of UCD; it has frequently been used to describe the early years of the college (M. Tierney (Ed.)(1954) *Struggle with Fortune* Dublin, Browne and Nolan).

more so in the post-independence and post-war period, was such that there was no need to subvert the provisions of the Act in order to provide an overwhelming Catholic sensibility in the college.

McCartney, in his history of UCD, paints a vivid picture of the Catholic life of the college and of the country in the first half of the century:

> It was inevitable ... that there would be a big physical presence of priests in UCD in its first sixty years or so. It also followed that there would be a strong Catholic ethos among its staff and students, for the strength of Catholicism in the college was no more than a reflection of its overwhelming presence in society as a whole; ... it was part of the atmosphere the country breathed.... It is not to be wondered at, therefore, that medicine and especially medical ethics, philosophy, politics, sociology, education, science, history and literature were all studied within the framework of the prevailing Catholicism.[12]

Given that there had been a transfer of staff and students from the Jesuit-managed University College to the new institution it is not surprising that there was a significant clerical presence among the teaching staff of the college. Of the original appointments to 36 professorships and 15 lectureships in the college, 5 went to Jesuit clerics and 3 went to secular clergy. While some of these staff members continued in office into the 1940s, McCartney notes that in each case, they were replaced on retirement by lay persons.[13]

As was to be expected, the student body was initially, and continued to be during this period, overwhelmingly Catholic in its religious affiliation. McCartney[14] gives a figure of 98 per cent for the proportion of Catholics among those who stated their religion on registration in 1909–10 and observes that this figure was remarkably constant over the years, being 97 per cent in 1960–61. An interesting feature is that about 12 per cent of this 97 per cent were clerical students, religious sisters or religious brothers. Whereas most of the Catholic dioceses in the rest of Ireland sent their clerical students to Maynooth for their complete clerical education and formation, the Dublin Archdiocese used UCD as the source of the initial higher education of its clergy.

---

12 McCartney, op. cit., pp. 224–6.
13 Ibid. p. 161.
14 Ibid. pp. 168–9.

Large numbers of black-suited clerical students were, therefore, a significant visual and social component of life in the humanities departments of the college.

There was never a very significant clerical presence on the Governing Body of UCD. In the Governing Body formed in 1932, for instance, there were just 3 clerical members out of 34—one of them nominated by the government, one elected by the graduates and one co-opted member, the latter two being professors in the college.[15]

UCD and national politics

Given the history of the struggle for the establishment of a university for Irish Catholics and the resistance to that struggle by Trinity College and its unionist allies, it was, perhaps, inevitable that nationalism would be a significant element in the life of the new UCD. In the pre-1908 UCD, the President, Fr Delaney, had been anxious to avoid antagonising the government and jeopardising the struggle for a satisfactory university settlement. Nevertheless, the students, on occasion, expressed their nationalist sentiment, most dramatically by intervention at the graduation ceremonies of the Royal University which prevented the playing of the national anthem. In the turmoil of the Great War, there were divided philosophies, so that whereas some of the more prominent leaders of university opinion fought and died in France, more stayed at home and participated in the 1916 Rising and the subsequent War of Independence. Among those whose names were prominent in these events were Tom Kettle, Professor of National Economics, who was killed at Ginchy in September 1916; Thomas MacDonagh, Professor of English, who was executed in Dublin after the 1916 Rising; Eoin MacNeill,[16] Professor of Irish, who

---

15 By contrast, the Governing Body of UCC at that time had 4 clerical members including 3 bishops, while UCG had 10 clerical members including 6 bishops. Four of these 9 bishops were nominated to the governing bodies by their local authority constituencies. It may also be noted that Trinity was not free from the attraction of the clerical collar. The first Provost of Trinity chosen after the 1908 Act—John Pentland Mahaffy—was an ordained minister of the Church of Ireland while the next holder of the position—John Henry Bernard—had resigned from his position as the Protestant Archbishop of Dublin in order to assume the provostship in 1919.

16 Eoin MacNeill (1867–1954), Professor of Irish in UCD, was the leader of the Irish Volunteers. He was the father-in-law of Michael Tierney, President of UCD from 1947 to 1964.

was leader of the Irish Volunteers and who was imprisoned after the Rising, and two UCD students, Kevin Barry and Frank Flood,[17] who were executed during the War of Independence.

A revealing view of student aspirations at that time is provided by some of the contributors to the centenary history of the Literary & Historical Society (L&H). George O'Brien (1892–1961), a student at UCD just before the Great War and later Professor of Economics, recalled:

> During my undergraduate years in University College, the prevailing opinion among the students was constitutional nationalism. . . . . Our interest in the parliamentary battle was not entirely impersonal. We all took it for granted that, if Home Rule was achieved, we would be among the politicians of the new Ireland. A Home Rule Parliament in those days would, no doubt have been dominated by the Irish Party, who would have earned the credit for its establishment. We in the College had many connections with the Irish Party. . . . The newspapers sometimes speculated regarding the future and constructed 'shadow cabinets' which contained many of our friends. We all confidently expected that in a short time we would be exercising our oratory, not in the dingy Physics Theatre in 86 [St Stephen's Green, Newman House] but in 'the Old House in College Green'.[18]

Following the establishment of the Irish Free State and the subsequent civil war (1922–3), the anti-treatyite Sinn Féin group never obtained a significant footing in UCD. In later years the college came to be identified with the Cumann na nGaedheal/Fine Gael party and a number of prominent members of the academic staff served as Dáil deputies and as Cabinet members in governments formed by that party.

The 1926 merger

As noted in Chapter 1 the Royal College of Science for Ireland[19] was formally established in 1867. The Albert Agricultural College began

---

17 Kevin Barry (1902–20) was a medical student at UCD. He was the first person to be executed in the War of Independence (1919–22). Frank Flood (1902–21) was a UCD engineering student who was executed in 1921.

18 Meenan, J. F., (Ed.) (2005, 2nd edition). *Centenary History of the Literary and Historical Society 1855–1955*. Dublin, A. & A. Farmar, p. 113.

19 The 'Royal' prefix appears to have been dropped from common usage, even before the foundation of the Irish Free State in 1922 and the college was normally referred to simply as 'The College of Science'. This name for the buildings and the

its life in 1838 as the Glasnevin Model Farm. The College of Science provided professional education and training in science and engineering and theoretical education in agriculture. The Albert College, *inter alia*, provided practical agricultural training for students of agriculture from the College of Science. The Royal College was perceived to be particularly favoured by the various British governments before Irish independence and this favouritism appeared to be confirmed when it was provided with imposing new buildings in Merrion Street, completed in 1911. It shared its buildings with the Department of Agriculture and Technical Instruction, the government department which oversaw its work.[20] The authorities in UCD, which had a School of Civil Engineering and a Faculty of Science (including technology and agriculture), but negligible funds to provide laboratories and other teaching spaces, were understandably jealous of their well-endowed neighbour.

On the establishment of the Irish Free State in 1922, the new government established itself in those sections of the College of Science building on Merrion Street which had formerly been occupied by the Department of Agriculture and Technical Instruction. However, with the outbreak of the Civil War in 1922, the threat to the security of the government required that the College of Science be closed. It remained closed after the end of the Civil War in 1923 and a vigorous debate was conducted in the new Dáil and in the newspapers on what its future might be. As early as the summer of 1922, UCD had set up a committee to prepare its case for the acquisition of the College of Science. Although the case made by UCD was compelling, it was particularly fortunate in that the new Minister for Education was one of its own professors, Eoin MacNeill.[21] Despite some mild protests

---

educational activities conducted in them persisted long after the college had been absorbed into UCD; it was even used in the 1926 Act which transferred ownership of the college to UCD. Senior members of the UCD staff were still trying to have engineering and science students refer to their home as 'Science Buildings' rather than 'the College of Science' even into the 1960s.

20 Vincent McCabe, a former Dean of the Faculty of Engineering and Architecture at University College, Dublin, is writing a history of the Royal College of Science and its absorption into UCD. He has allowed the author access to some of the papers he has collected in the course of this work. Among the details he has revealed is that the workshops of the College of Science were used as a munitions factory for the army during the 1914–18 war.

21 MacNeill's successor as Minister for Education was another UCD professor, John Marcus O'Sullivan.

from representatives of Trinity and UCG and from graduates of the College of Science, an Act was finally introduced in the Dáil in 1926 which transferred the College of Science and the Albert College to UCD.[22] Proposals from UCC that it should be permitted to develop its agricultural facilities were more persuasive than those from Trinity and the Act also provided for the establishment of a Faculty of Dairy Science in University College, Cork.

The acquisition of the College of Science by UCD may be seen more as a 'takeover' than a merger. The UCD Faculties of Science, Engineering and Agriculture moved in to occupy the premises of the College of Science and the Albert College. Although staff from the College of Science were taken on as staff members of UCD there is evidence that they were not treated very generously by their new employer.[23]

Growth and development of UCD

UCD had 530[24] students registered in its first year of operation, 1909–10. The numbers grew rapidly as the following table illustrates:

Table 2.1 Numbers of full-time matriculated students registered in UCD 1909–31

Period	Numbers
1909–10	458
1915–16 to 1919–20*	1,079
1920–21 to 1924–5	1,232
1930–31	1,542
1938–9	1,998
1948–9	2,862
1955–6	3,220
1959–60	3,961

*These figures are average annual figures for the quinquennial periods.
Sources: *Commission on Higher Education Report* Vols 1 and 2 (1967), p. 47; Corcoran, op. cit., (1932) p. 110

22 The substantial buildings of the Royal College of Science in Upper Merrion Street in Dublin which became the home of the UCD Engineering School and some of its science departments in 1926 much later became the main home of the Irish government.

23 The writer, as a 24-year-old graduate of UCD with two years' post-graduate study, was appointed as a staff member in the Engineering School in 1959 on the same grade as that of a fellow staff member who had transferred from the staff of the College of Science 33 years previously.

24 The figure of 530 registered students includes a number of non-matriculated students.

By the 1960s UCD had 1,600 more enrolled students than its perceived rival in Trinity College. In terms of accommodation for the student body, however, the picture was rather different.

The 1908 Act had provided a sum of £150,000 as a combined capital provision for the National University and University College, Dublin. On its foundation, UCD had a long-term lease of the home of the old UCD on St Stephen's Green. It was also given the premises of the Royal University on Earlsfort Terrace. It proceeded to build on the Earlsfort Terrace site, although, because of various difficulties, financial and otherwise, the building plan agreed was never completed. Significant additional teaching space was provided with the acquisition of the College of Science and Albert College in 1926 and, in 1933, the college purchased the estate of Belfield as an athletic ground for its students.

Dr Michael Tierney

Michael Tierney had been appointed as President of UCD in 1947 and remained in office until 1964. He was an ardent believer in the importance of the college and an articulate spokesman for that belief. He had strong views on the appropriate role of staff[25] and students in the college and became embroiled in frequent rows with the premier student debating society, the L&H, which traced its history back to Cardinal Newman. His close links with Dr John Charles McQuaid, the Catholic Archbishop of Dublin,[26] throughout his presidency, were unapologetically deployed in fostering the Catholic ethos of the college. He presided forcefully over a major expansion of UCD, both in terms of staff and student numbers, and in the diversity of its academic offerings. In his actions on behalf of UCD he saw Trinity as its rival and gloried in the fact that his college had, by that time, far outstripped Trinity in terms of student numbers. His greatest achievement undoubtedly was to convince the government of the need to move UCD to Belfield, and in the successful development of the new university campus which, by the time of his retirement, was well on its

---

25 See FN 40.
26 John Charles McQuaid (1895–72) was Archbishop of Dublin from 1940 to 1972. A conservative thinker, for much of that period he was seen as the leading figure in the Irish hierarchy

way to accommodate the major part of the UCD community.

Student numbers expanded substantially in the post-war period. A cartoon in the satirical magazine, *Dublin Opinion*, at this time showed the Minister for Education presenting Dr Tierney with a shoehorn 'to enable him to get another four or five hundred students into UCD.'[27] Eventually, in the 1950s a consensus emerged within UCD that the only feasible option was to relocate the college to the suburban site at Belfield.[28]

There was considerable public opposition to this plan and it was debated at length in newspapers and pamphlets of the day. A pamphlet produced by the discussion group Tuairim, for example, saw the plan as both unnecessary and undesirable and put forward an alternative scheme involving the purchase of various buildings in the vicinity of Earlsfort Terrace.[29] The government appointed a Commission to consider the Belfield plan and, also, accommodation needs in UCC and UCG. The Report of this Commission, which was chaired by Justice Cearbhall Ó Dálaigh, recommended acceptance of the plan and this was accepted by government.[30] The first building on the Belfield campus, the Science Building, was completed in 1963.

Inevitably, Tierney's forceful reign as President led to the growth of an opposition camp within and without the college. Within the college there was a small but articulate group of senior staff who resented the autocratic manner of his administration. The wider body of staff and, significantly, the junior staff in the various assistant grades, may have occasionally resented his manner but were supportive of his achievements. Outside the college, liberal opinion saw him as the quintessential representative of an older, conservative group in Irish society—as the lay mirror image of Archbishop McQuaid. The liberal voice was, however, very faint in the Ireland of the time; it tended to manifest itself mainly in the columns of *The Irish Times*.

---

27 McCartney (op. cit., pp. 227–76) describes the unsuccessful efforts made by the college during the presidency of Dr Tierney to expand its accommodation on the Earlsfort Terrace site.

28. In some documents of the time, the site is referred to as the Belgrove site.

29 Tuairim, (1960). University College Dublin and the Future. Dublin, Tuairim.

30 *Report of the Commission on accommodation needs of the constituent colleges of the National University of Ireland* (1959).

The staff at UCD

Section XII of the charter of UCD described the manner in which the academic staff of the college—the professors, lecturers, assistants and demonstrators—were to be appointed. In essence, professors and lecturers were to be appointed by the NUI, it having obtained advice from the college; assistants and demonstrators could be appointed by the Governing Body of the college, without reference to the NUI, and would hold office for such periods as the Governing Body prescribed. Assistants were further described in this section of the charter as assistants to the professors and lecturers. Demonstrators were not defined in any way but were to be seen as occasional lower-level teachers with duties confined to assisting in laboratory and other practical classes.

From 1920–21, the staff numbers gradually increased, as shown in Table 2.2.

Table 2.2 UCD staff numbers classified by grade 1920–48

Session	Professors	Lecturers	Assistants
1920–21	47	7	22
1930–31	55	28	21
1940–41	60	42	23
1947–48	62	51	42

Source: Data extracted from *Calendars of University College, Dublin* 1920–60

It can be seen that the academic community of the college was built around the professoriate with similar but smaller numbers of lecturers, appointed by the university, and a small number of assistants, appointed by the college, to assist in its teaching function. The assistants were normally recent graduates who, if they planned an academic career would aspire to be promoted to the 'statutory' grades of professor or lecturer.[31] The increase in the number of assistants recorded for the 1947–8 session corresponds with a significant increase in student enrolment in the later years of that decade (see Table 2.1).

At the end of the 1940s a change developed in the staffing structure, as shown in Table 2.3

---

31 Arising from the fact that their appointment required the creation of a statute, lecturers came to be known in UCD as 'statutory lecturers'. The terms 'statutory' and 'non-statutory' came to be used informally to distinguish between those appointed by the university and those appointed by the college. This distinction became particularly significant when, towards the end of the period under review in this chapter, UCD created new positions of assistant lecturer and college lecturer.

THE IRISH UNIVERSITY INSTITUTIONS 1908–60

Table 2.3 UCD Staff numbers classified by grade 1947–59

Session	Statutory		Non-statutory		
	Professors	Lecturers	College lecturers	Assistant lecturers	Assistants
1947–8	62	51			42
1950–51	61	41		24	33
1953–4	63	40	2	32	42
1956–7	67	34	19	32	71
1958–9	67	27	41	21	114

Source: Figures extracted from the *Calendars of University College, Dublin 1920–60*

In the 1949–50 session 21 persons were appointed to positions entitled assistant lecturer and in the 1953–4 session, two persons were appointed to positions entitled college lecturer. In addition, in the 1955–6 session, the Governing Body had approved the appointment of a college professor although the person selected did not take up the position.[32] No such titles were mentioned in either the Charter of the NUI or the Charter of UCD.

An unwelcome visitor

At the meeting of the Governing Body of UCD on 24 June 1959, it was reported that a letter had been received from John Kenny,[33] an assistant in the Law Faculty, in which he stated that 'unless the Governing Body were prepared to disclaim any power to appoint college professors, college lecturers and assistant lecturers he proposed to petition the Government to appoint a Visitor to decide this matter.'[34] The essence of his complaint was that the college had no power to create such positions and that it was acting *ulta vires* in so doing.

The position of the President, Dr Tierney, and the Governing Body might be summarised as follows. The college required a growing number of assistants to cope with the rapidly increasing student enrolment. It was desirable to have an appropriate promotion system in place for these assistants. The terms 'college lecturer' and 'assistant lecturer' were merely titles used to distinguish between different stages in the promotional structure for assistants. Moreover, it was claimed, the complexities and delays of the NUI system of appointment to

32 The writer was appointed as an assistant lecturer in the 1959–60 session.
33 Kenny in later years was a distinguished member of the Irish Supreme Court.
34 UCD Governing Body Minute Books in UCD archives, GU2/22.

lectureships was such that the creation of additional lectureships as an alternative to the increase in the number of assistants would seriously inhibit the college in its efforts to increase academic staff numbers to cope with the increase in student numbers.

The opposing view was that the actions of the President—and of a compliant Governing Body—were part of a plan to subvert the intentions of the framers of the NUI charters who had planned a university system wherein the academic staff members were free from presidential control and were protected in the exercise of their academic freedom by the terms of those charters. Dr Tierney, it was claimed, was intent on having a body of academic staff who would be dependent on him for their tenure and who would, consequently, not oppose his views. The decrease in the number of lectureships in the college [35] was cited as additional evidence in this regard. This view was expressed most trenchantly by Dr Noel Browne TD in a subsequent debate in Dáil Éireann.[36]

The Secretary of the Governing Body, J. P. McHale,[37] responded to Mr Kenny's letter stating that:

> ... the alleged illegality of the title 'College Lecturer' and 'Assistant Lecturer' has been before the Governing Body and the Senate of the National University on a number of occasions. The Governing Body [...] being satisfied as to the position decided not to change a practice which it believes to be entirely proper and which has been in operation to the great benefit of the College for a considerable time. The Senate has also decided by Resolution to take no action.[38]

This response of McHale was approved by the Governing Body at its meeting on 24 June. Kenny consequently presented his petition to

---

35 See Table 2.3 above. The number of lectureships had dropped from 51 to 27 over the period since Dr Tierney assumed the presidency.

36 Dáil Reports 28 April, 1960.

37 J. P. McHale was a long-term officer of the college having served under three presidents from 1954 to 1987. In addition to his role as Secretary of the college he was its Bursar and its Supervisor of Examinations. In his letter dated 21 May 1959 rejecting Kenny's request, McHale wrote: 'The President has instructed me to enquire whether you think it altogether proper that you, as an Assistant in the College, should query the actions of the Governing Body in a matter which does not appear to him to be any direct concern of yours'(*Report of the Board of Visitors on University College, Dublin* 1960, p. 6).

38 UCD Governing Body Minutes 24 June 1959, UCD archives, GU2/22.

the government which responded promptly by establishing a Board of Visitors on 6 November 1959.[39]

The institution of the Visitor is one peculiar to the British legal system. Traditionally, charitable foundations, a category that included the old universities and their colleges, included in their structures the office of the Visitor who would, conventionally, be a representative of the founder or of the monarch. The function of the Visitor was to exercise an internal judicial function to ensure that the terms of the charter were being adhered to. Importantly, a decision of the Visitor was final and could not be appealed to any superior court outside the institution.[40] The 1908 Universities Act established the monarch as the Visitor for the new university and its colleges; this function was assumed by the state on its foundation in 1922.

The Report of the Board of Visitors was published on 29 April 1960.[41] It was a complete vindication of the position taken by John Kenny in his petition and a rejection of the arguments put forward by the college. The Board found, *inter alia*, that 'The Governing Body appointed college lecturers and assistant lecturers at all times aware that it was at least doubtful that it was authorised so to do, and on the basis of a belief that the possibility of legal action being taken to question the regularity of such appointments was remote'. Simultaneously with the publication of the report, the government published the terms of the University College Dublin Bill, 1960, whose object was to indemnify the authorities in UCD against any action which might be taken arising from the report and to validate the appointments already made, as a temporary measure.[42]

There was a heated, if brief, debate in the Oireachtas on the Bill. Noel Browne, a long-term critic of Michael Tierney, used the debate in the Dáil to talk of 'the disreputable activities of the President …

---

39 The members of the Board of Visitors were: Mr Justice George Murnaghan, Mr Justice Thomas Teevan and Judge Michael Binchy.

40 Costelloe, Kevin (1994–5) ' The University Visitor: a local Employment Court'. *Journal of the Irish Society of Labour Law* Vol. 10, pp.12–29. Costelloe examines the extent to which the prerogatives of the Visitor under the British legal system could be applied under Irish constitutional arrangements.

41 Although invited to do so by the Board of Visitors, none of the assistants, other than the petitioner, made a submission to the Board.

42 University College Dublin Act 1960. No 16 of 1960.

[who] has usurped the powers of the Senate to make appointments' and stated: 'There is an obvious reason for the usurpation of this power and it is that there is an individual autocrat avid for power who wished to absorb as much as possible into his own hands by hook or by crook.' He went on:

> The findings of this report are, I believe, inextricably bound up with the Belfield project which was recently discussed in this House. It is a fact that the gradual acquisition and abuse of the tremendous power and patronage by the University in the past ten or 15 years had as its main purpose—the obvious purpose was common jobbery—the forcing through of his personal ambition to remove the college from the city and have it built in the Belfield area. In order to suppress any contrary opinions, any opposition there might be to this project, he proceeded to institute a reign of fear—fear of insecurity of appointment—by the devices to which he resorted[43]

In the Seanad, Professor Michael Hayes, an elected NUI senator and a professor in UCD, made a lengthy defence of the administration in UCD and argued that their actions were not illegal.[44] *The Irish Times*, in its editorial columns, stated ominously that there remained 'a number of rather frightening questions which the Minister, quite understandably, was anxious to avoid, and which were given rather too political a complexion by the few members of the Dáil who had the courage to mention them.'[45]

The University College Dublin Bill was passed without amendment and the college adjusted the titles given to the 'non-statutory' staff. [46] The resentment of the senior members of the college at the

---

43 Dáil Reports, 28 April 1960, col 306.

44 Seanad Éireann Debates, 2 and 3 June 1960.

45 *The Irish Times*, 30 April 1960. *The Irish Times* at that time would not have been seen as a friend of UCD. Its attitude towards the college may be seen in an editorial published later that year, on 11 November, on the university situation in Dublin, where it stated: 'Ideally, of course, one would not dare to compare the university course with that of any vocational institute. In practice, however, it seems that UCD which, perhaps unkindly, has been called "a glorified technical school" even by some of its own graduates, has failed to give to many of its students the comprehensive education which alone distinguishes the university from the technical college.'

46 The writer received a letter appointing him as Assistant Lecturer in July, 1959. In July 1960 and 1961, he was re-appointed as Assistant II. In July 1963, he was appointed as Assistant II (Assistant Lecturer) and in December 1964 he was appointed as Assistant I (College Lecturer). The title Assistant III was given to those appointed at the lowest Assistant grade.

manner in which they had been dealt with by the Board of Visitors and at the way they had been pilloried in the Oireachtas debates was long-lasting.

The Irish Federation of University Teachers

In 1897, an Association of Intermediate and University Teachers (AIUT) was established in Cork.[47] The association aimed to represent the 'assistant masters of the various Intermediate and University establishments in Ireland.' The association was short-lived, however, and after the establishment of the NUI in 1908, and the setting up of the Association of Secondary Teachers of Ireland in 1909, the AIUT ceased to exist. It was not until the 1960s that steps were taken again to develop an organisation that would represent the views of academic staff in Ireland.

In Britain, the Association of University Teachers (AUT) had been formally established in 1919 to promote the cause, initially, of the junior teaching staff and later of all academic staff.[48] In Ireland, the setting up of the Commission on Higher Education in 1960 was the catalyst for the establishment of a similar body to represent the views of academic staff in the Irish universities.

Inevitably, it was in UCD, under the autocratic presidency of Michael Tierney, that the first moves were made. As explained earlier, the governing body structures established by the 1908 Universities Act, did not allow for any direct academic staff representation, other than for the professors. Occasionally, non-professorial staff members did become members of the governing body through election by the graduates but this was not seen by them as an adequate mechanism to provide representative membership. It was not only on the governing body that membership was limited; even at faculty level, membership of college faculties was confined to statutory officers of the university, i.e. professors and 'statutory' lecturers. These restrictions were not seen to be unduly oppressive when the number of non-statutory staff was small. However, with the expansion of student and staff numbers in

---

47 Marie Coleman (2000) *IFUT—A History*. Dublin, Irish Federation of University Teachers.

48 Harold Perkin (1969). *Key Profession—The History of the Association of University Teachers*. London, Routledge & Kegan Paul.

the 1950s and the deliberate reduction in the number of statutory lectureships, the numbers of non-enfranchised staff grew very rapidly. As can be seen in Table 2.3 above, the proportion of non-statutory staff to total academic staff grew from 28 per cent in 1948/9 to 65 per cent in 1958/9. Many of these non-statutory staff members, particularly in the new 'college lecturer' grade, were people of significant seniority and academic stature. There was a growth, therefore, in the number of unrepresented academic staff with a particular interest in the reform of university governing structures.

The announcement of the establishment of the Commission on Higher Education in 1960 was the spur for the first recruiting call for members of the proposed new Academic Staff Association (ASA) whose initial role would be to represent the views of the general body of academic staff to the Commission. The association was to be open to all full-time members of the academic staff, despite some initial suggestions that its membership should be confined to non-professorial staff. The ASA very quickly built up a substantial membership so that, by the time it made a submission to the Commission in 1961 it had recruited almost three quarters of the academic staff as members.

The move to establish a representative body for staff in UCD was quickly followed in UCG and in UCC and in 1963 discussions commenced between the associations with a view to establishing a national federation of staff associations. These moves came to fruition with the establishment of the Irish Federation of University Teachers (IFUT) in 1966. IFUT was to be a federation of staff associations in each of the university colleges but was also to allow individual membership.[49]

The situation in Trinity was different in a number of ways to that in the colleges of the NUI. Although there were occasional voices calling for an extension of the franchise, there was not such a strong sense of disenfranchisement among the staff in Trinity as there was in UCD. There were, in addition, arising from the variety of staff grades with different entitlements, a number of different constituencies which had not come together in a single representative organisation but which occasionally formulated their collective view. The junior Fellows sometimes issued statements as junior Fellows; at other times, the Fellows as a whole expressed their collective view. For the body

---

49 Coleman, op. cit.

of non-Fellow academic staff members, the Readers and Lecturers Association (RLA) was their representative body. It was the threat to the whole Trinity community, which was perceived in the merger announcement, which led to the establishment of an Academic Staff Association (ASA) in the college in 1967 to represent the mind of the whole academic staff, as had happened in the NUI colleges. The new ASA was immediately successful in recruiting a large number of the staff from all categories as members and it was, from the beginning, recognised as one of the branches of IFUT.

IFUT was to have a significant role in the debates and negotiations which were to take place relating to the merger proposals. Its identity as a professional body concerned with general policy issues in university education gave it a status in the public arena which, for a time, at least, was seen as equally important as that of the universities as corporate bodies or as that of university presidents and provosts.

Trinity College, Dublin 1908–1960

The 1908 Universities Act was a very significant achievement for Catholicism and nationalism in Ireland; it may also be seen as a significant achievement for Trinity College, Dublin. Dublin University, and its single college Trinity, were left undisturbed in their privileged positions as the well-endowed university of the Protestant ruling class in Ireland.[50] Before the First World War its student numbers were about 1,300 and its total income was about £90,000—including some £60,000 from its endowments.[51]

Trinity College had a form of government, surviving since 1627, which, while similar to the models in Oxford and Cambridge, was anomalous when compared to the 19th-century models evident in London and, now, in Dublin. These newer models might be characterised as 'democratic' having provision for internally elected presidents, and for governing bodies which had directly elected members of the professoriate and of the graduates, representatives of local authorities,

---

50 The new Queen's University in Belfast was seen as the appropriate home for Presbyterian students.

51 McDowell and Webb, op. cit., pp. 499–510. By comparison, there were 605 students in UCD in the 1910–11 session and its annual grant, as set out in the 1908 Act, was £32,000.

and nominees of the monarch/government. In Trinity, by contrast, where academic staff were divided into Fellows and non-Fellows, all power was vested in the Fellows who comprised the body corpporate of the college and thus were legally the owners of the college. They were recruited, when vacancies arose, by open examination in mathematics, classics, Hebrew, philosophy and physics,[52] and, if successful, were appointed for life. When the college required teachers whose expertise lay outside the somewhat narrow confines of the fellowship examination professors were appointed but these professors had no role in the government of the college.

The Fellows were further sub-divided into Senior and Junior Fellows. The Board of the college, its governing body, consisted of the seven Fellows most senior in terms of their appointment to fellowship, together with the Provost—a Crown appointee. Academic staff who were not Fellows were not members of the college but, rather, employees of the college although the Board had also, as members, elected representatives of the Junior Fellows and of the non-Fellow professors.

At the turn of the century there had been considerable agitation within the college for reform to these governing structures and the matter had been considered by the Fry Commission in 1906. The Commission proposed that there be a fully elective board. However, its proposals, on this matter, as on the question of providing a solution for Catholic higher education, came to nothing. Luce, in his history of Trinity College,[53] describes the controversy as follows:

> Constitutional reform in the College had more and more come to mean change in the composition of the Board. So far as the Fellows were concerned, the recruitment of its members, apart from the Provost, by seniority alone had become the central issue, but the reforming party was motivated by the practical consideration that promotion to senior fellowship had become excruciatingly slow, rather than by the argument that the mechanism was wrong in principle.[54] The body of non-Fellow Professors,

---

52 Recruitment to fellowship by annual open examination continued until 1916. Luce, J. V. (1992). *Trinity College Dublin—The first 400 years*. Dublin, Trinity College Dublin Press, p. 138.

53 Luce,.op. cit., p. 124.

54 McDowell and Webb (op. cit.) note that in 1896, the youngest of the Senior Fellows was 69 years old. Fifty years later, the same situation prevailed as noted by

now equal in size to that of the Fellows, had a different ground for complaint, in that they could not even aspire to a seat on the governing body.

Eventually a scheme was arrived at whereby the Board was to be augmented by the addition of two elected representatives of the Junior Fellows and two elected representatives of the professors. This arrangement was put in place by the issuing of Letters Patent in 1911.[55] The 1911 settlement survived, more or less unchanged, until the end of the century.

Political change

Trinity had been apprehensive about the likely advent of home rule in the period leading to the Great War of 1914–18. What came in 1922 was much more traumatic with the establishment of the Irish Free State. Trinity had been, unashamedly, a bastion of Protestantism and unionism in Ireland. It feared that henceforth, it would be part of a small isolated community in danger of being over-run by a triumphalist Catholic majority.

A few days after the Anglo-Irish Treaty was agreed in 1921, the board of Trinity passed a resolution expressing the hope that the university's representatives in Westminster would support the settlement since 'the true interests of Trinity College can only be furthered by Irish peace, and in building up happier conditions in Ireland the Board believes that Trinity men should take an active and sympathetic part'. McDowell and Webb note, however, that the resolution was only passed by 9 votes to 3, being opposed by a number of extreme conservatives.[56] This cautious approach to the changed circumstances was to characterise Trinity's stance over the succeeding decades.

McConnell in his evidence to the Commission on Higher Education.(*Commission on Higher Education 1960-67 Report* (1967) Vols. 1 and 2, p. 435).

55 The issuing of Letters Patent or King's Letters was a mechanism whereby, if a change to the statutory basis of the institution was not deemed to be fundamental in character, it could be enacted by a letter from the Privy Council, without the necessity of going through parliament in Westminster. The 1911 Letters Patent, in addition to the changes in the composition of the Board, gave the college a great deal of autonomy in the regulations of its own affairs, including the right to alter the provisions of the Letters Patent; this move was seen as a re-assurance to the college in view of the expected, and feared, arrival of home rule.

56 McDowell and Webb, op. cit., p. 430.

A QUESTION OF IDENTITY

Terence Brown, a modern Trinity Fellow, sums up the situation within Trinity at that time as follows:

> The most unhealthy aspect of the College's situation was its growing isolation from the main currents of national life. While UCD was making significant contributions, TCD retreated into its shell, and let events pass it by. In this it was reflecting the ghetto mentality that was tending to envelop the Protestant community in the South. It has been well said that the College in the centre of Dublin took on 'a striking resemblance in social terms to the Big Houses of the countryside—each symbolising a ruling caste in the aftermath of its power'.[57]

The first official dealings of the college with the new Irish government were in relation to finance. A generous financial settlement with Trinity had been promised in the Government of Ireland Act of 1920. This commitment was not replicated in the terms of the Treaty. Although a settlement was reached in relation to some outstanding commitments arising from the Land Acts, the attitude of the new government officials to the college was seen to be quite hostile and so no further approaches relating to finance were made by the college to the government for the next 23 years. As McDowell and Webb note: 'This [attitude] had its craven side; at times the College was afraid to request some trivial and technical concession from a government department for fear of focussing attention on itself and provoking a debate in the Dáil '.[58] The caution went to the extent of the board prohibiting the members of the college writing from the college to the public press on religious or political matters which could be seen as controversial.[59]

As an illustration of the prevailing sentiment in Trinity after the Irish Free State was established, the custom continued, at the end of college dinners, of toasting 'The King' rather than 'Ireland'. McDowell and Webb record that in 1930, when the then auditor of the College Historical Society called for a toast to Ireland following the inaugural meeting of the session, the society was forbidden the use of the com-

---

57 Brown, T. (1981). *Ireland—A social and cultural history 1922–79*. London, Fontana. p. 115.
58 McDowell and Webb, op. cit., p. 429.
59 Ibid. p. 430.

mon room until it had purged its contempt.[60] It was not until 1945 that the toast to 'The King' was finally dropped from college occasions. The same ambiguity applied to the playing of the national anthem in college. It was not until 1939 that the playing of 'God save the King' was omitted from the rubrics at the annual Commencements ceremony.

The question of which flag to fly in the college raised similar difficulties. At first, it was decided to continue with the flying of the Union flag but a compromise was soon arrived at whereby the Irish tricolour was flown at one side of the college façade, the Union flag at the other side and the college flag in the middle. This practice continued until 1935 when the Irish colours were granted their appropriate recognition. However, trouble arose in 1945 when a group of Trinity students, in celebrating the end of the war in Europe, raised the flags of the victorious allies—including the Union flag—on the front of the college. This was taken as a provocation by a group of Republican-minded students from UCD who proceeded to burn the Union flag in front of the college. The Trinity students retaliated by burning the Irish tricolour; the disturbances which ensued continued for two days.[61]

It should be noted that Trinity was not alone in Ireland in facing conflicts of loyalty in the period after the foundation of the Irish state. Such ambiguities were not uncommon in private and commercial life in Ireland in the first half of the century; Trinity's difficulties may have been the most public manifestation of them.

The student body

It is difficult to get an authoritative figure for the number of students attending Trinity in the first two decades after 1908. The figure of 1,300 quoted previously from McDowell and Webb was obtained by accumulating the annual matriculation figures for the college—a method believed by them to give the most accurate available number.[62] More reliable figures for later years are obtained in the report of the

---

60 Ibid. p. 434.

61 In reporting on the collateral damage during the disturbances, *The Irish Times* noted that windows had been broken in Jammet's Restaurant. *The Irish Press* reported that the windows of *The Irish Times* had been smashed.

62 McDowell and Webb, op. cit.; p. 499.

Commission on Higher Education (Table 2.4).

Table 2.4 Student numbers at Trinity College Dublin 1938–65

	1938/9	1948/9	1955/6	1959/60	1964/5
Total student numbers	1,543	2,236	1,651	2,443	2,909

Source: Extracted from Table 23 of the Commission on Higher Education *Report* (1967) Vols. 1 and 2

The temporary peak in the numbers in the 1948–9 period may be explained by a surge in the enrolment of overseas student in the period immediately after the ending of the 1939–45 world war. This is illustrated in figures given by McDowell and Webb for the national origins of matriculating students in different years (Table 2.5)

Table 2.5 Birthplace of Trinity students expressed as a percentage of the total

Year of matriculation	26 Counties	Six Counties	Total Ireland	Great Britain	Other overseas
1911–13	68	16	84	10	6
1922–8	69	17	86	8	6
1938–9	56	25	81	11	8
1945	53	30	83	11	6
1946	46	22	68	18	14
1947–51	33	21	54	29	17

Source: Figures from Table 2 in McDowell and Webb, 1982, p 505

An extension of these figures into the 1960s can be obtained from broadly comparable data supplied to the Commission on Higher Education in 1966 (Table 2.6)

Table 2.6 Home residence of Trinity students expressed as a percentage of the total

Year	Republic of Ireland	Northern Ireland	Total for Ireland	Great Britain	Elsewhere
1964/65	41.0	20.9	61.9	31.2	6.9
1965/66	41.2	23.3	64.5	28.3	7.2

Source: Figures from Table 92 in the Commission on Higher Education *Report* (1967) Vols. 1 and 2

McDowell and Webb also give the figures for the religious affiliation of matriculating students in different years (see Table 2.7).

Table 2.7 Religious affiliation of Trinity students expressed as a percentage of the total

	Church of Ireland	Other Protestant	Catholic
1910	75	15	10
1925	52	28	20
1950	51	27	22

Source: Figures extracted from Fig. 3 in McDowell and Webb, 1982, p. 504

The ban on Catholics attending Trinity

The picture presented in the preceding sections is of an institution which was peculiarly remote and distant from its surroundings. Whereas some part of this isolation was a conscious choice on the part of Trinity itself, some of it was undoubtedly due to the attitudes of the majority population outside the walls. In particular, the stance of the Catholic Church with regard to the attendance of Catholic students at Trinity must be seen to have had a significant bearing on the development of the Trinity community.

As was noted previously, the Synod of Thurles in 1850 had issued a condemnation of the 'godless' Queen's Colleges which had been established a few years earlier. In 1875, in the wake of the removal of religious tests in Trinity by Fawcett's Act of 1873, that condemnation was extended to Trinity College Dublin. Statute 333 of the 1875 Synod warned the faithful 'that they should abstain from frequenting [the Queen's Colleges], lest their faith be tainted by any stain or lest they be infected by any pestiferous doctrine'. Statute 334 stated:

> We have deemed it necessary to make the same provisions concerning attendance at the non-Catholic Dublin College, namely that of the Most Holy Trinity [as for the Queen's Colleges], and with all the more reason in that there has recently been introduced in to that academy a system of purely secular education.[63]

This condemnation was elaborated at the Synod of 1927 and then, from the Synod of 1956, Statute 287 declared:

> With regard to the College of the Most Holy Trinity in Dublin we forbid:

---

63 Irish Federation of University Teachers (IFUT) archives, 5.21. In 1970, IFUT published a significant document detailing the history of the ban and arguing for its removal. These excerpts from the synodal documents are reprinted from the IFUT document.

1) Catholic youths to frequent that college; 2) Catholic parents or guardians to send to that college, Catholic youths committed to their care; 3) Clerics and religious to recommend in any manner parents or guardians to send Catholic youths to that college or to lend counsel or help to such youths to frequent that college. Only the Archbishop of Dublin is competent to decide, in accordance with the norms and instructions of the Holy See, in what circumstances and with what guarantees against the danger of perversion, attendance at that college may be tolerated.[64]

Dr John Charles McQuaid, Catholic Archbishop of Dublin at that time, was zealous in his enforcement of these prohibitions and in his re-statement of them in his Lenten pastoral letters from year to year. 'The ban', as it was popularly called, was to remain until 1970.

In the light of these episcopal prohibitions, therefore, the figures quoted above of some 22 per cent of the Trinity student body declaring themselves as Catholic in 1950, can be seen as some evidence of a waning of the authority of the Catholic Church in relation to educational matters. Some of that 22 per cent would undoubtedly have been accounted for by the 67 per cent of the student body which had been born outside the 26 counties at that period but that proportion is unknown. Nevertheless, it is obvious that the ban was at least partly responsible for the anomalous position of Trinity, even at the end of the period under review in this chapter.

A modern-day Provost of Trinity, Dr William Watts, gives a revealing personal view of this period in the history of Trinity:

> It is hard now [2008] to realise how far Trinity had been excluded from Irish life. The hostility of the Roman Catholic Church, especially shown by John Charles McQuaid as Archbishop of Dublin, meant that few Catholic students were present and they were mostly from outside Ireland or outside the Dublin diocese. The Protestant population was small, and too small to sustain a university, but the College was enriched by the aftermath of World War II: British ex-servicemen, some British school-leavers, often with family connections with Ireland, Nigerians and other colonials soon to achieve independence, and many others; students from Northern Ireland were specially significant. Older Trinity graduates speak with nostalgia of the diversity and international character of the student body at that time. The British presence meant that, when George VI died in 1952 and Elizabeth was proclaimed to be monarch, British students stood up at the end of Commons and sang 'God save the Queen'. . . . I

---

64 Ibid.

see it now as a last expression of a dying past from which Trinity had to move on.[65]

The situation of Trinity College in 1960 is illustrated usefully in evidence given to the Commission on Higher Education by the Provost of Trinity, Dr A. J. McConnell.[66] In a lengthy statement, the Provost, *inter alia*, said the following:

> I think it is true to say that after the new State was set up, the College lacked a good deal of self-confidence and did not quite know what its position was going to be in the new regime. I think that it was not at all sure whether the new Ireland wanted it or not, and I may say that at the time the governing body of the college consisted predominantly of older people who had been brought up in a totally different regime and who, while not antagonistic to the new regime at all, had not been of that way of thinking and therefore felt out of touch. I think that there was a time for nearly twenty years or more when the College was very uncertain of itself. For the last 15 years, at least, I would say from my own experience that the College has had a feeling of confidence that the country does need Trinity College and needs the contribution that Trinity College can make.[67]

In a written submission to the Commission the Trinity Board stated that the Board would welcome the appointment of a Dean of Catholic students and would be glad to make land available for the erection of chapels in addition to the existing Church of Ireland chapel.

University Colleges Cork and Galway 1908–60

The 1908 Act incorporated the Queen's Colleges in Cork and Galway into the National University. Thus, Queen's College, Cork (QCC), founded in 1845, became University College, Cork (UCC), and Queen's College, Galway became University College, Galway (UCG), two constituent colleges of the new university. This marked the third phase in the life of the colleges, they having been initially constituent colleges of the Queen's University and then, after 1882, independent teaching institutions preparing students for the examinations of the Royal University. The colleges had laboured under the episcopal ban

65 Watts, W., (2008) *William Watts—A Memoir* Dublin, Lilliput pp. 39–40.
66 Albert McConnell was Provost of Trinity from 1952 to 1974.
67 Commission on Higher Education, op. cit., Vols 1 and 2, p. 435.

on attendance at the 'godless' Queen's Colleges and then had suffered when the establishment of the Royal University opened up competition for students from a wide variety of non-university institutions. They were now to face competition from their new partner in Dublin.

UCC in the NUI

With the election of a Liberal government in 1906 and the probability that university legislation would, at last, be brought forward to satisfy Catholic and Nationalist aspirations, a campaign developed in Cork to have Queen's College Cork established as an independent University of Munster.[68] This campaign, which was led by the recently appointed President of the college, Bertram Windle, became the focus of intense local passion and received support from local newspapers and politicians and from local authorities in the Munster area. However, the national mood indicated that a national solution—eventually incorporated in the federal NUI—would be contained in the new Act.

Although Windle took an active part in the Dublin Commission, of which he was a member, and in the Senate of the new university, and welcomed the new status of UCC in the NUI, he was to come back again with his plans for an independent University of Munster at the end of the 1914–18 war. In 1919 he was asked by the government to draft a Bill for the proposed university. However, by this time, the university question in Cork had become an intensely political one with Sinn Féin supporting the NUI and attacking Windle for his threats to the integrity of the new National University.[69] The NUI Senate also vigorously opposed the move to independence for UCC. At a time of increasing unrest in Ireland, the British government soon lost any interest it had in the project and did not proceed with the Bill.

Windle resigned from the presidency after the defeat of his efforts and thus left Sinn Féin as the dominant political voice in the college.

---

68 Munster, in this campaign and in the provisions of the 1908 Act, finished at the River Shannon; County Clare was seen as being in the sphere of influence of University College, Galway.

69 Windle (1858–1929) came from an Anglo-Irish family and was a convert to Catholicism. He was attacked as a 'Castle Catholic' and was criticised by Sinn Féin for talking to the British government when a Sinn Féin government had been established. He resigned from the presidency when his plans for the University of Munster were defeated. (Murphy, op. cit., pp.201–7).

However, despite the strong support for the NUI in the battle on the University of Munster question, there was still within the college a certain resentment at the perceived dominance of the Dublin representatives on the Senate of the NUI. It was felt that a proposed development in Cork, or in Galway, would not be approved unless UCD agreed, whereas a proposal coming from UCD was sure to be accepted.

Religion in UCC

Although Queen's College Cork had suffered from the episcopal ban on the attendance of Catholic students, it would appear that the ban was not honoured in Cork to the same extent as elsewhere. Thus, it was proudly reported by the President in 1882–3 that 61.2 per cent of the student body were Catholic compared with 34.4 per cent in 1870–71, despite the re-statement of the ban by the Synod of 1875.[70] Nevertheless, the ban, followed by the widening of access to university qualification through the examinations of the Royal University in 1882, limited its opportunities for growth.[71]

With the formation of the National University and the non-extension of the ban to the NUI colleges by the Catholic hierarchy, the inevitable Catholicisation of the college took place. By the time of the presidency of Alfred O'Rahilly[72] Murphy notes that, as in UCD, the number of non-Catholic students was negligible. He quotes O'Rahilly in 1944 stating:

> ... in spite of the liberalistic bias of our foundation, [we do not] believe in higher education divorced from sound philosophy and religion. Our students are 97% Catholic and we do not intend to ignore this fact. Negative un-denominationalism does not appeal to us in Cork.[73]

The change of the college from secular Queen's College to *de facto* Catholic University College was symbolised in 1934 by the replacement of the statue of Queen Victoria on the Aula Maxima by one of

---

70 Murphy, op. cit., p. 109.

71 There is some evidence reported by Murphy that the ban was more effective in deterring women students than their male counterparts.

72 President 1943–54.

73 Murphy, op. cit., p. 277. O'Rahilly became a priest of the Holy Ghost congregation in 1955 on his retirement from the presidency.

St Finbarr, sculpted by Cork sculptor Séamus Murphy.

In terms of student enrolment, the high point of the Queen's College was reached in the early 1880s when over 400 students were registered in the college. The establishment of the Royal University regime in 1882 led to an immediate drop of 25 per cent in the enrolment figures and this drop continued until, at its lowest point in 1886–7, the enrolment was just 107. Critics described the college as merely a glorified medical school and there was considerable justification for this criticism; Murphy reports that in 1899 there were 137 medical students in Queen's College, Cork with only 34 in arts and science, 17 in engineering and 7 in law.[74]

The advent of the NUI in 1908 and the consequent end of the ban on Catholic students attending UCC brought the expected turnaround in its fortunes. In its first full year as a constituent college of the NUI, 1910–11, the student numbers had risen to 404 and by 1918 the numbers reached 530. By 1960, the number of students registered had reached 1,304.

UCG in the NUI

University College, Galway, unlike its sister college in Cork, welcomed the advent of the NUI unreservedly and saw it as its saviour, at a time when the college's continued existence had been questioned. In particular, the umbrella of a large national university gave credibility to its academic awards when its size and limited facilities might have brought them into question. Apart from occasional complaints about the Dublin dominance of the affairs of the NUI, and the irritation of travel to meetings which were always held in Dublin, this affection for the NUI persisted throughout the century even when its fellow constituent colleges were harbouring disaffection.

Development of UCG

Queen's College, Galway was the smallest of the three Queen's Colleges in terms of student enrolment. As shown in Table 1.1, it had an annual average of 153 students on its books in the 1869–79 period compared with a figure of 253 for Cork and 400 for Belfast. As for the other colleges, the change to the Royal University regime brought

74 Ibid., p 152.

drastic reductions in its student numbers; Mac Mathúna reports that enrolment dropped from an average of 86 in the 1872–81 decade to 34 in the 1882–91 decade. With the changes brought about by the 1908 Act, he cites a growth from 133 in 1908–9 to 260 in 1923–4 and then an almost three-fold growth from 1921 to 1932.[75] By the 1959–60 session, its student numbers had risen to 945.

These figures conceal a worrying period in the life of the college in the first two decades of its life as an NUI institution. The fall in student numbers following the establishment of the Royal University had led to a serious drop in the college's income—and in the salaries of the professors whose income was partly related to the number of students registered for the courses they gave. This financial concern was exacerbated by the terms of the 1908 Act which allotted an annual grant of £12,000 to UCG compared to a sum of £18,000 to UCC. In order to make up this deficit the college, in 1912, developed a proposal whereby the county councils represented on its governing body would contribute a total sum of £1,500 per annum to the college, on foot of a promise from the Chancellor of the Exchequer of a matching, non-statutory, grant of £2,000 per annum. This was agreed by the county councils and, although it led initially to an assumption by some local authority members that their grant gave them the right to interfere in the internal affairs of the college, it did lead to a closer identity between the college and the people in its catchment area.

Despite this development, there were still serious financial difficulties for the college. Thus, there was alarm in the college when the 1926 Bill proposing the transfer of the Royal College of Science and the Albert College to UCD made new financial arrangements for UCD and UCC but made no change in the allocation to UCG. Indeed, in 1923 the payment of the non-statutory grant was deferred and a submission from the college to the Minister for Education referred to the low salaries in UCG relative to those in the other colleges and a recurrent deficit of some £2,000. A deputation from the college to the government found itself dealing with a Minister for Finance, Earnán de Blaghd,[76] who was not very sympathetic to their approaches. In a

---

75 Séamus Mac Mathúna 'National University of Ireland, Galway' in Dunne, (Ed.) op. cit., p. 279.

76 Earnán de Blaghd (Ernest Blythe) (1889–1975) was a Northern Protestant who

speech to the Dáil in 1926, de Blaghd said:

> [UCG] are quite in earnest about the question of getting money, but I do not know that they are at all in earnest about the question of doing special work which would entitle them to money.... If Galway is not going to do special work, then frankly as far as I am concerned I do not think that it would be a wise course ... to maintain it as a sort of toy college ... [77]

While it appears from this passage that the possibility of shutting down UCG had been considered in government circles, the particular 'special work' which de Blaghd, an Irish language enthusiast, had in mind was that the college should become a place where the teaching would be carried out through the medium of Irish. Although UCG was located in a city which was estimated at the time to be 40 per cent Irish speaking and with a hinterland which was 80 per cent Irish speaking, the college had not considered such a proposal previously. Its particular concern with the proposal that it should become, primarily, a provider of courses taught through Irish was that the number of Irish-speaking secondary school students who would qualify for matriculation to the college would be so small that the college would not be viable. Nevertheless, it finally came to an agreement with the government in 1926 that it would accept the thrust of the government proposals, supported by a series of measures to increase its annual grant, improve salaries, employ Irish-speaking staff, reduce fees and establish a special scholarship scheme for Irish-speaking students.

The 1926 agreement provided a clear identity for the college and gave a basis for its development over the coming decades. There were significant resource implications in the plans adopted in that, in most cases, parallel lectures had to be provided in Irish and in English; in later years staff in UCG complained that the sums agreed in 1926 had not altered although the value of money had decreased substantially. The requirement that staff appointed to the college be competent in the Irish language most probably had an effect on the ability to recruit

---

became involved in Irish nationalist politics in the early 20th century, was a Minister in the Sinn Féin provisional government and in the first Irish Free State government. He was very active in the movement for the revival of the Irish language and in Irish language cultural affairs. He later became the Director of the Abbey Theatre.

77 Mac Mathúna in Dunne (Ed.), op. cit., p. 73.

dence given by the individual colleges.[23] This evidence largely mirrored the attitudes of the colleges discussed in Chapter 2. Thus, UCD was in favour of the dissolution of the NUI, UCG was in favour of its retention and UCC was ambivalent on the issue. In summarising the arguments made in favour of retention, the Commission listed them as follows:[24]

> a) The system has advantages, especially in the making of appointments and the maintenance of standards;
> b) The colleges, as parts of a system, are protected from undesirable pressures to which they might be subject as separate institutions;
> c) Dissolution of the system would involve difficulties, whereas the preent system has been working reasonably well;
> d) The system contains potentialities for co-operation through such expedients as the establishment of shared professorships, co-ordination of research effort, interchange of staff, and equality of salaries and superannuation benefits;
> e) The system offers particular benefits to provincial colleges.

However the Commission concluded:[25]

> a) That the N.U.I., as a whole, works rather as a loose aggregation of colleges than as an integrated system;
> b) That its organisation is inadequate and unsuited to the work which it has to carry out;
> c) That in regard to courses and examinations, the University function has tended to wither and that the colleges have, in practice, assumed University functions;
> d) That the appointments system in the University is slow and cumbersome;
> e) That the University has not acted as a force for co-operation or co-ordination, either within its own system or outside it.

The submissions of Dr Tierney on behalf of UCD appear to have particularly impressed the Commission.[26] Although the Report was published after he had left office as President, its endorsement of

---

23 Commission on Higher Education, op. cit., *Report* Vols. 1 and 2, pp. 405–26.
24 Ibid. p. 408.
25 Ibid pp. 411–12.
26 The written submissions of Dr Tierney are available in Box 7150 in the Manuscript Room in Trinity College Dublin. His oral evidence is referred to by the Commission at various points in the Report.

his views must have been very satisfying after the humiliation of the report of the Board of Visitors a few years earlier.

Trinity College, Dublin

The Commission looked at the position of Trinity College in the Irish higher education system from a somewhat different perspective than that employed in its analysis of the NUI. On the one hand it appeared somewhat reluctant to disturb the equanimity of an institution which had close links with the minority religious population and with the North of Ireland. It seemed particularly disinclined to involve itself in the conflict between TCD and UCD which was described so colourfully by Michael Tierney in his evidence to the Commission. On the other hand, given that its main driving force was the growing demand for university places in Ireland and that the student body in Trinity was characterised by a high proportion of non-Irish students, it looked closely at Trinity's plans to expand its overall numbers.[27]

Any analysis of the make-up of the student body in Trinity had, of course, to take into account the prohibition by the Catholic hierarchy on the attendance of Catholic students there. Although, as noted previously, some Catholics did ignore the prohibition, its persistence had a major influence on the ability of Trinity to recruit more Irish students; in effect Trinity was drawing the primary body of its Irish students from what was then a small, and diminishing, cohort of non-Catholic families.

The Commission made no judgemental comment on the ban and simply recorded a lengthy statement from one of its episcopal members, Dr Philbin, which explained the Catholic position. On the assumption that the ban would remain in place, however, it expressed serious concern about the appropriateness of plans to increase the number of student places from 2,999 in 1965/6 to 4,000. It assumed that the majority of the extra students would necessarily come from outside Ireland at a time when there was a grave shortage of places and resources in the institutions catering particularly for the majority population. It recommended, therefore, that Trinity should be required

---

[27] In Table 2.6 above it can be seen that in 1965/6, 35.5 per cent of the student body enrolled in Trinity had home residence outside the island of Ireland; 58.8 per cent had home residence outside the Republic of Ireland.

staff from the widest possible field.[78] Nevertheless, the college grew over the next decades and developed particular areas of excellence related to its location. It did not have significant difficulties regarding accommodation and new buildings until the end of the period under consideration in this chapter.

In summary, therefore, by 1960 there were two universities, four university colleges and the recognised college in Maynooth offering university education in the Republic of Ireland. None of them were particularly secure financially[79]; UCD in particular faced a major accommodation crisis. The number of students seeking admission to the colleges was beginning to increase substantially. In Dublin, the two largest of the institutions, UCD and Trinity, were locked in what Michael Tierney referred to later, in oral evidence to the Commission on Higher Education, as 'a truceless cold war'. The majority of students attending Trinity College had home residences outside the state—about equal numbers from Northern Ireland and from Great Britain. It was against this background that the government, in 1960, decided to initiate the first comprehensive analysis of the Irish higher education sector since the foundation of the state.

78 The procedures put in place required that, if more than one applicant for a position was considered to be qualified for a position being filled, a qualified applicant deemed to be competent in the Irish language would be preferred to one deemed not competent.

79 Trinity had survived on its endowments until 1947 when it finally approached the Irish government for an annual grant. Despite its fears, Mr de Valera, the Taoiseach at the time, acceded to their request without conditions, and an annual grant of £35,000 was conceded.

Éamon de Valera on his first visit to the NUI as President of Ireland (2nd left) with (l–r) college presidents Monsignor Pádraig de Brún (UCG), Henry St John Atkins (UCC) Michael Tierney (UCD) and NUI Registrar Seamus Wilmot (Irish Press)

3. The Commission on Higher Education

During the debate on the University College Dublin Act, the Minister for Education, Dr Patrick Hillery, had referred to his intention to establish a Commission on Higher Education to which the difficulties in UCD would be referred. This was a reiteration of a promise which he had made during a debate on the Report of the Commission on the NUI colleges' accommodation needs. The public announcement of the formation of the Commission was made in October and it held its first meeting on 8 November 1960.

Chief Justice Cearbhall Ó Dálaigh was named as the Chairman of the Commission. Its members, numbering 28, included such prominent representatives of Irish industry as C. S. (Todd) Andrews and General M. J. Costello, of international academia as the Cambridge historian Herbert Butterfield and University of Manchester economist Charles Carter, along with a number of Irish academics and a selection of bishops. Its terms of reference were set down as:

> Having regard to the educational needs and to the financial and other resources of the country, to inquire into and to make recommendations in relation to university, professional, technological and higher education generally, with special reference to the following: a) the general organisation and administration of education at these levels; b) the nature and extent of the provision to be made for such education; c) the machinery for the making of academic and administrative appointments to the staffs of the Universities and University Colleges; and d) the provision of courses of higher education through Irish.[1]

In his inaugural address to the Commission, the Minister told the members that they were limited only by the Constitution of the state in the scope of their investigations.

The reference in c) above regarding the machinery for making appointments in the universities arose, obviously, from the controversy over appointments in UCD. Apart from that, the terms of reference were extremely open and wide-ranging and allowed the Commission

1 Commission on Higher Education *Presentation and Summary of Report*, p. 1.

to inquire into every aspect of the operation of every institution of higher education in the state. This it duly, and somewhat laboriously, proceeded to do.

During the lifetime of the Commission, two other investigative bodies studied different aspects of Irish education. In October 1962, the Minister for Education, in co-operation with the OECD, appointed a survey team whose report was titled *Investment in Education*.[2] The terms of reference for this survey related primarily to the preparation of an 'inventory of the existing position in relation to skilled manpower.'[3] Although the survey team, under the direction of Professor Patrick Lynch, concentrated its efforts on the position at primary and secondary levels, there was a certain overlap between its work and the terms of reference of the Commission.

Then in 1963, the Taoiseach, Seán Lemass, appointed another OECD-sponsored survey team, whose report was titled *Science and Irish Economic Development*,[4] again under the direction of Professor Lynch. The major aims of this survey were 'to supply information on the present state of research and technological development in the Irish economy and, using suitable criteria, to forecast the likely growth of these activities over the next fifteen years.'[5] Again, inevitably, there was some overlap between the work of this group and the terms of reference of the Commission.

Despite these possible overlaps the Commission 'did not institute any formal relationship with either [survey] team since their functions and ours were essentially different, even though, in the event, our findings may prove to be complementary.'[6] In the event, there was no significant clash between the reports of the survey teams, published in 1965, and the report of the Commission when it was eventually published in 1967. There was, however, a clash with the recommendations of another group dealing with technical education.

In 1963, the Minister for Education, Patrick Hillery, had announced

---

2 *Investment in Education: Report of the Survey Team appointed by the Minister for Education in October, 1962*, (1965), Dublin, Stationery Office.
3 Ibid., p. xxix.
4 *Science and Irish Economic Development* (1965), Dublin, Stationery Office.
5 Ibid., p. xi.
6 Commission on Higher Education, op. cit., p. 2.

the establishment of a limited number of regional technological colleges (RTCs).[7] Their brief, as initially envisaged, was to provide the facilities for a proposed new Technical Schools Leaving Certificate programme. Although the plans for a new Leaving Certificate were eventually dropped, the proposed new colleges developed a certain educational and political momentum. The educational rationale for the colleges was altered so that they were to provide for a greatly expanded technician education, a need for which had been shown by the *Investment in Education* report. The political rationale for them was that they were seen as providing significant future investment in those towns which were mentioned as possible locations for the new colleges.

The new Minister for Education, Donogh O'Malley, established a steering committee on technical education in September 1966. Its brief was to advise the Minister generally on technical education but with particular emphasis on the development of the proposed RTCs. This was a development which was to provide a significant alternative view to that of the Commission on some aspects of higher education but its establishment so late in the life of the Commission meant that, again, no significant relationship developed between the two bodies.

The work of the Commission

The Commission sat from 1960 to 1967. In its summary report, it detailed the exhaustive nature of its workload.[8] Having invited submissions directly from a wide range of persons involved in higher education and from the general public through newspaper advertisements, it received 245 written submissions which it estimated to amount to 1.1 million words. In addition, it took oral evidence from 138 witnesses representing 40 different bodies, and from 16 other individual witnesses. It estimated that the transcript of the oral evidence amounted to 1.6 million words.[9] The Commission, or members of it, visited higher education institutions in Ireland, Britain and six other European countries. In its summary report, the Commission described its role as being the first commission since the foundation of the state

---

7 White, T. (2001), *Investing in People—Higher Education in Ireland from 1960 to 2000*. Dublin, Institute for Public Administration. p. 50.

8 Commission on Higher Education, op. cit., pp. 4–5.

9 Ibid.

to inquire into higher education generally. The Report continued:

> Within [the Report's] compass had to be contained findings on many diverse questions, and we could not choose to deal only with topics that attracted most immediate interest. We have had to consider not only immediate problems but also long-term needs. We therefore attempted to frame recommendations that would be valid far beyond the present.[10]

The unlimited brief which the Commission set for itself undoubtedly contributed to its longevity.[11] The extent to which the approach of Chief Justice Ó Dálaigh as Chairman contributed to its seven-year span can only be speculated upon. His lawyerly approach to the terms of reference given to the Commission does seem to have ignored the growing pressures on the existing system and the government's wish for speedy and clear-cut solutions. Undoubtedly, successive Ministers for Education were embarrassed by repeated Dáil questions as to the expected date of the publication of a report from the Commission.

This impatience on the government's part came to a head in Dáil Eireann in December, 1966 when the Parliamentary Secretary to the Taoiseach, Mr Carty, used the occasion of the vote on the Estimates to attack the Commission's tardiness. In his contribution he stated:

> We have had sitting here for the past six years a Commission on Higher Education. It is about time they brought out their report. We are fed up listening to replies to Dáil Questions that it will be out soon, that it will be out next month and so on. If they are not able to bring out their report soon, the Commission should be abolished. . . . I understand—I do not know how true it is—that the Minister was told either directly or indirectly that if he referred to proposals for university education in any form, the Commission would resign. I say to the Minister: Let them resign and be damned to them.[12]

This surprising attack on the commission from the government benches was repudiated by the Taoiseach, Jack Lynch, in a public statement a few days later. He stated that the deputy was not a member of

---

10 Ibid. p.7.

11 The seven-year span of the Commission's work might be compared with the work of the Robbins Committee which sat from 1961 to 1963. Its brief, was 'to review the pattern of full-time higher education in Great Britain and in the light of national needs and resources to advise Her Majesty's Government on what principles its long-term development should be based.'

12 Dáil Reports Vol. 225, cols 225–6, 1 December 1966.

the government and did not speak for the government and added that he was satisfied that the Commission had not threatened to resign. The *Irish Independent*, in reporting on the Taoiseach's statement, speculated that this could be a sign that the recently appointed Taoiseach might be about to bring about a new, tougher, disciplinary approach in the Fianna Fáil party and that this repudiation of his parliamentary secretary was a new departure for an Irish political leader.[13] In fact, as White reports, the action of the Taoiseach was in response to a threat from Cearbhall Ó Dálaigh that he would resign as Chairman if the Taoiseach did not publicly disassociate himself and the government from Mr Carty's comments.[14]

The report was finally published in 1967, firstly in a *Presentation and Summary of Report*, given to the Minister for Education in February and published on 22 March, and then in the main two-volume report of 976 pages of which the first volume was issued in August of that year.

Philosophical assumptions of the Commission on Higher Education

Ireland was not unique in subjecting its higher education system to a detailed analysis in the 1960s. The huge growth in the demand for greater access to the university at this time was a worldwide phenomenon which forced governments and other bodies to examine both the financial implications of expansion and the changes which might be required in the institutions arising from such a transformation.

In the United States, Clark Kerr, having been dismissed from his position as President of the University of California at the behest of Ronald Reagan, the newly elected Governor of California, was

---

13 *Irish Independent* 6 December 1966. *The Irish Times* did not comment editorially but printed a letter from an E. G. Head on the same day which complained, with tongue in cheek: 'Sir, I wish to point out the absence of regularity in the announcement of the appearance of the report of the Commission on Higher Education. I think that last year it was July and this year September and the Minister for Education has just announced February for 1967. Might I suggest that it would be more convenient for those interested if one month were added for each year. Thus, it would be March for 1968, April for 1969 and so on coming round to February again in 1979. It would also be interesting and, if one might be permitted to say, encouraging if the names of the members of the commission who had died off in the previous year were published at the same time.'

14 White, op. cit., p. 43.

invited to chair the Carnegie Commission on Higher Education.[15] The Commission, which sat for seven years, examined the US higher education system under six broad headings:

- Social justice
- Provision of high skills and new knowledge
- Effectiveness, quality and integrity of academic programmes
- Adequacy of governance
- Human and financial resources available to higher education
- Purposes and performance of higher education institutions.

The Commission's thinking was published in a number of authoritative reports whose major outcome was seen in the Higher Education Act passed in 1972.

In Ireland, the international study that was most closely studied was the Robbins Committee Report on higher education in Great Britain.[16] This report, published in 1963, set out a detailed set of assumptions on which the Committee based its thinking. It stated that there were at least four objectives essential to any properly balanced system of higher education, and continued[17]:

> We begin with instruction in skills suitable to play a part in the general division of labour. We put this first, not because we regard it as the most important, but because we think that it is sometimes ignored or undervalued. We deceive ourselves if we claim that more than a small fraction of students in institutions of higher education would be where they are if there were no significance for their future careers in what they hear and read....
>
> Secondly, while emphasising that there is no betrayal of values when institutions of higher education teach what will be of some practical use, we must postulate that what is taught should be taught in such a way as to promote the general powers of the mind. The aim should be to produce not mere specialists but rather cultivated men and women.
>
> Thirdly, we must name the advancement of learning.... the search for truth is an essential function of institutions of higher education and the process of education is itself most vital when it partakes of the nature of discovery....
>
> Finally there is a function that is more difficult to describe concisely, but that is none the less fundamental: the transmission of a common culture

---

15 Carnegie Commission on Higher Education (1972). *A Digest and Index of Reports and Recommendations, December 1968–June 1972*

16 Lord Robbins (1963). *Higher Education: Report of the Committee appointed by the Prime Minister under the Chairmanship of Lord Robbins*. London, HMSO.

17 Ibid., pp. 6–7.

and common standards of citizenship.

By contrast, the Irish Commission on Higher Education did not explicitly list in its report the aims which it saw as the basis for its analysis of the Irish higher education system. It did not even quote Newman, reference to whom had been *de rigueur* in Irish writing on universities. At best, such aims must be inferred from the recommendations of the Commission in relation to particular institutions or systems of institutions, or from its summary conclusions. The final section of its Summary Report states:

> The central theme in our recommendations regarding the general provision to be made for higher education, at a time of unprecedented increase in the demand for it, is the necessity to ensure that academic standards will be maintained and safeguarded. Standards are vital in higher education. Standard-setting must come from the top. The universities therefore have a pre-eminent role in the safeguarding of standards. Universities can fulfil their purpose only if they are enabled to teach to the highest standard and are active in carrying out and promoting fundamental research in the humanities and sciences.
>
> What must be done to ensure that standards are safeguarded? There are we believe, only two courses of action open:
>
> (1) Severe restrictions could be imposed on numbers entering the universities, and this would lead to a better staff/student ratio and to an improvement of facilities. If no substantial increase in public spending on the universities were to be forthcoming, this is the expedient we would recommend.
>
> (2) Given adequate financial support there could be immediate expansion of staff and facilities to match resources with present student numbers, followed, as further staff and facilities become available, by a regulated expansion of student numbers. This we believe to be the proper course.[18]

In commenting on this dominant role assigned to the universities by the Commission it should be noted that in 1965/6 the universities and the teacher training colleges combined represented some 78 per cent of the total number of students in the state system of higher education.[19] The great expansion in higher education facilities outside the universities was to come in the years after the Commission

---

18 Commission on Higher Education, op. cit., *Presentation and Summary of Report*, pp. 97–8.
19 Commission on Higher Education, op. cit., *Report* Vols. 1 and 2, p. 26.

reported.[20]

Whatever the rationale for the recommendations of the Commission, they were very university-friendly and they proposed a model of the university which could fit comfortably into the intellectual framework proposed by Newman a century earlier. Among its other recommendations, the Commission proposed that the length of the primary degree course be standardised at four years rather than three, that entry standards be raised, that staff student ratios be improved to a value of 1:12, that provision for post-graduate education be given a much greater importance, that academic staff appointment systems be improved and that university teachers have half the working year free for study and research.[21] Understandably, academic opinion was very favourable to this emphasis of the Report. More controversially, the Commission made a number of recommendations with regard to the broad, institutional structure of university education in Ireland; these were to provide fuel for much debate over the following months.

The Report lists 37 specific recommendations for the development of the higher education system in Ireland. These range from the most far-reaching—such as the dissolution of the NUI—to the relatively minor—such as the recommendation that the Irish Folklore Commission be established as an institute within UCD. The recommendations which deal most directly with a possible merger are considered in the following sections.

The National University of Ireland

The first and, in the light of the history of university education in Ireland, the most dramatic recommendation of the Commission was that 'U.C.D., U.C.C. and U.C.G. should be established by Act of the Oireachtas as independent universities to replace the N.U.I., with provision for the special position of St. Patrick's College, Maynooth.'[22] In its investigation of this issue, the Commission analysed the evi-

---

20 A lasting legacy of the Commission for the benefit of future historians is the set of 191 tables in the Report which provides a comprehensive database on the conditions in the Irish higher education sector in the middle of the 20th century.
21 Commission on Higher Education, op. cit., *Presentation and Summary of Report*, pp. 94–5.
22 Ibid., p. 94.

over a period of time to reduce the proportion of foreign students in its student body to the same level as that in the other university colleges, with the assumption that this would lead to an overall reduction in student numbers.

The other feature of Trinity College which the Commission looked at was its form of government. As discussed above, the college had retained a governing structure which might have been seen as more appropriate to an antique Oxbridge college than to a university/college system which was larger than any of those colleges. There were no outside members on its Board nor were there any representatives of the general body of staff. The Commission saw no justification for this exceptionalism on the part of Trinity and recommended that it should have governing structures similar to those it was proposing for the newly independent NUI colleges.

Structures of university government

The 1911 settlement had allowed Trinity to make some changes to its ancient governing structures. However, power still rested to a considerable extent with the seven senior Fellows thus providing a gerontocratic form of government to the college. Submissions to the Commission from the Board conceded that it was 'not, perhaps, as representative as it might ideally be. . . . it was hoped to increase the representation of the younger people into the Board.' Moreover, the college submitted that it would like a limited number of outside representatives on the Board.[28]

The colleges of the NUI, on the other hand, had seen no changes to their governing structures since 1908 and there was a pent-up demand by the academic staff for change. As we have seen, the establishment of the commission in 1960 had stimulated the formation of the Academic Staff Association (ASA) in UCD in 1960, to act as a representative body for all the academic staff in the college. Within a few years, this led to the formation of similar bodies in the other colleges, including Trinity College, and to the founding of the Irish Federation of University Teachers (IFUT) in 1963 as a federation of the various staff associations.[29] The ASA in UCD, perhaps because of

28 Commission on Higher Education, op. cit., *Report*, Vols. 1 and 2, p. 504.
29 Coleman, M. (2000). *IFUT—A History*. Dublin, Irish Federation of University Teachers.

the perceived autocratic nature of the presidency of Michael Tierney, was to the fore in pressing for reform of its governing structures. Its proposal to the Commission for a reformed Governing Body envisaged a body much reduced in size, with substantial decreases in the representation of graduates, and government and local authority representatives, and increased representation of academic staff, including non-professorial staff.[30]

The Commission proposed radical changes to the existing arrangements. Its members believed that there were two major interests to be accommodated in the governing bodies. They stated that 'the majority of members should be drawn from the academic staff and a substantial minority—not less than one-third—from outside the university.'[31] They further proposed that whereas the professoriate must be in a majority, the lecturing staff should have a reasonable representation. They saw no merit in the representation of graduates or of local authority members and proposed that outside members should only be appointed directly by central government. Neither did they see any place for students on the governing bodies. Finally, they proposed that governing bodies should be much smaller than in the existing models; they proposed that the membership should be between 9 and 17. All these arrangements were to apply equally to Trinity and to the new universities formed from the NUI constituent colleges.

For the new 'ex-NUI' universities, it was obviously necessary to consider the disposition of the authority which had previously been exercised by the Senate and the General Board of Studies of the NUI. Apart from matters connected with academic staff appointments, this authority was primarily concerned with purely academic affairs; it was therefore proposed that the new academic authorities should be the primary recipients of these powers. Apart from this consideration, the Commission did not make any positive recommendations regarding the highest academic authority in the universities other than to indicate their preference for much smaller bodies than the existing NUI

30 Commission on Higher Education, op. cit., *Report*, p. 504. The Commission noted that although the statutory provisions in UCD allowed for only six representatives of the academic staff out of a total of 34 members on its Governing Body, in fact, through the variety of electoral mechanisms, there were at that time 20 current or recent members of staff on the Governing Body.
31 Ibid., p. 505.

academic councils. They suggested a membership of about 25 which 'should be representative of the main categories of studies pursued in the university ... should include representatives of the full-time lecturing staff as well as the professorial staff and its membership should be open to renewal at regular intervals.'[32]

In its proposals for new governing structures, the Commission does not appear to have consulted any models other than those proposed by staff in the existing Irish university institutions. Universities governed by bodies with a majority of academic staff were almost unknown in the English-speaking world, other than in Oxford and Cambridge. The Robbins Committee, for example, sitting at the same time as the Commission, considered and dismissed proposals for such a body on the grounds that:

> ... it is in general neither practicable nor justifiable that the spending of university funds should be in the hands of the users. Academic autonomy is more likely to be safeguarded where the public has a guarantee that there is independent lay advice and criticism within the universities .... We are sure that teachers have an important contribution to make to the discussion of the non-academic affairs of their institutions and we are therefore much in favour of their adequate representation on ultimate governing bodies. But we are in agreement with the principle of a majority of lay members on the Court or Council.[33]

As with some of its other proposals, the Commission's recommendations might be criticised for lack of intellectual breadth and as being excessively influenced by the arguments coming from the existing university institutions in proposing governing bodies with academic staff majorities.

The Commission considered the possibility of joining Trinity and UCD in a single, new, university.[34] It is not clear from its report what, if any, submissions were made on this matter. The arguments in favour of such a merger would have centred on the grounds of the efficiencies likely to be achieved in a merged institution. Undoubtedly, there would also have been some reference to the history of Trinity College and its role as a pillar of the unionist establishment in Ireland. These

---

32 Ibid., p. 510.

33 Robbins op. cit., pp. 217–18. The term 'lay member' is generally used in the British context for those who are not members of the staff of the university.

34 Commission on Higher Education, op. cit., *Report*, pp. 416–17.

notes are evident in a reservation to the commission's report made by General Costello[35] and they were usually heard in discussion on the amalgamation issue both inside and outside the universities at the time.

Whatever the nature of the discussion which took place within the Commission on this issue, the final Report firmly rejected the idea of a merger between Trinity and UCD and concluded:

> The association of the two colleges on equal terms in a new university would mean some diminution of status, actual or potential, on the part of both colleges. These considerations would probably be less significant if there were a long-standing tradition of inter-institutional co-operation between UCD and TCD. But in the absence of such conditions, the association of two institutions in a new university would not be a natural and easy evolution from the existing relationship. It would represent the enforced combination of two institutions described by the former President of UCD [Tierney] as having been in 'a state of truceless cold war'.[36]

Moreover, it pointed out the apparent illogicality of releasing UCD from the shackles of one federal arrangement only to tie it to another one.

The Limerick University question

As recorded in detail by White,[37] a persistent theme in Irish educational debate since the 19th century was the demand by various groups in Limerick for a university or university college to be established there. Limerick had lost out to Galway in the 1840s as a location for one of the Queen's Colleges and this loss was confirmed by the establishment of the Queen's College in Galway as one of the constituent colleges of the NUI in 1908. The demand had continued with varying degrees of intensity after 1908 and became most focused with the establishment of the Limerick University Project Committee in 1959. The setting-up of the Commission in 1960 provided a focus for the committee and

---

35 Ibid, pp. 891–6. General Costello had been a prominent member of the national army from the foundation of the State and, subsequently a widely respected industrialist.

36 Ibid, pp. 416–17.

37 White, op. cit. In his chapter titled 'Limerick Wants a University', White explores the political debates on this issue during the 1950s and 1960s.

it made various written and oral submissions to it. In these submissions it made the case for the establishment of a full university college in Limerick which would have full faculties of Arts, Celtic Studies, Commerce, Science, Engineering, Medicine and Agriculture. In addition the committee engaged in continual lobbying of Limerick's local political representatives so that much of the clamour in Dáil Éireann over the non-appearance of the Commission's report had come from Limerick members.

The Commission, however, rejected the Limerick demands. It concluded:

> There is no national need at present for another university college. A university college in Limerick would satisfy a local demand, but the most urgent national need is that the existing university colleges should be adequately financed so that their teaching and research may be maintained at a proper level. To divert monies that might be available for this purpose to the establishment—in Limerick or elsewhere—of another university college which would be subject to the same deficiencies as the existing colleges would be to worsen a situation that already endangers the standards of our higher studies.[38]

St Patrick's College, Maynooth

Shortly after the establishment of the NUI in 1908, St Patrick's College, Maynooth had been accepted as a recognised college of the university. As such, it had participated fully in the life of the university and had been accepted, *de facto* if not *de jure*, as an equal party in its workings. If the Commission were to propose the abolition of the NUI, what would happen to the university linkage of Maynooth?

Contrasting with the prescriptive tone of the Report in dealing with other university institutions, the Commission adopted a *laissez faire* approach to the future of Maynooth. Deferentially, it declared itself as happy to accept whatever arrangements the episcopal trustees decided were most appropriate. The Commission described Maynooth's triune character as a seminary for the preparation of Catholic priests, a recognised college for the lay studies of these priests and a pontifical university for their theological formation, all three governed by a single, episcopal, Board of Trustees. However, it confined its consideration

---

38 Commission on Higher Education, op. cit., *Report*, p. 137.

of the future of Maynooth to that portion of the institution which was recognised by the NUI and in receipt of an annual state grant. It described Maynooth's position as a national seminary for the training of Catholic diocesan priests as its original and still its essential purpose.

In evidence to the Commission, the President of Maynooth expressed his satisfaction with the existing arrangements between the NUI and the college. He stated that 'in the event of dissolution of the NUI and the establishment of its constituent colleges as independent universities, he would think the college would seek to maintain the existing relations with UCD and to seek recognition from UCD in its new status.'[39].

A Council of Irish Universities

Having recommended the dissolution of the NUI and the continued independence of Trinity College, the Commission foresaw the need for a forum within which some co-ordination and rationalisation of university development might be achieved. It therefore proposed that a Council of Irish Universities be established on a statutory basis.[40] The Commission saw the need to build into any future system of higher education the means of securing greater communication and co-operation between the institutions of which it would be comprised, It proposed that the members of the new council would be the new independent universities in Dublin, Cork and Galway together with the University of Dublin and St Patrick's College, Maynooth 'if it should choose for itself the status of an independent university.'[41]

The proposed council, incidentally, was a much more substantial body than the analogous body in the UK, namely the Committee of Vice-Chancellors and Principals (CVCP).[42]

---

39 Ibid. p 423. Under the NUI arrangements, UCD acted as a 'guardian' or monitor of Maynooth on behalf of the NUI and professors and lecturers from UCD acted as internal examiners of their subjects in Maynooth.

40 Ibid. pp. 456–60.

41 Ibid., p. 458.

42 R. Aitken, (1968–9), 'The Vice-Chancellors' Committee and the UGC: Universities and the State', *Universities Quarterly*, Vol. 23, issue 2, pp. 166–71.

THE COMMISSION ON HIGHER EDUCATION

New Colleges

The most controversial of the Commission's proposals was that a new type of institution, titled the New College, should be established. In the summary of their proposals for this innovation they set out the functions which they saw the institution serving:

a) it would provide a new outlet for a growing demand for higher education;

b) it would offer a type and level of higher education suited to the country's educational needs;

c) it would extend access to higher education to greater numbers and beyond existing centres;

d) each New College would become a centre of intellectual and cultural life in its region;

e) the new institution would set a pattern for a more widespread provision of higher education in the future.[43]

The Report continued by noting that 'the New College would relieve the university of any obligation it may feel to meet the whole of the growing demand for higher education, and would enable the university to concentrate more of its efforts and resources on the attainment and maintenance of the highest standards of learning and scholarship.' It proposed that, initially, there would be two New Colleges, one in Dublin and one in Limerick, but that others should be provided in smaller centres when the demand materialised.

The New Colleges, therefore, were proposed primarily as a way of avoiding putting undue pressure on the existing university institutions and allowing them to maintain high standards, despite the expected pressure from an increase in the number of applicants to higher education institutions. They were to educate to pass bachelor degree standard and have strong commercial and vocational links. Their cost-per-student would be significantly lower than that in the university sector.

A Permanent Commission for Higher Education

At the time when the Commission was established, each university institution negotiated separately with the Department of Education

---

43 Commission on Higher Education, op. cit., *Report*, p. 127.

for its annual grant. There was considerable dissatisfaction with this mechanism. It was felt, on the one hand, that if such individual negotiation were to take place, it should be with the Department of Finance rather than with Education. More widespread was the view that there should be a buffer between the universities and government so that undesirable or improper political considerations and pressures would be avoided in the process of such negotiation; the model of the University Grants Committee (UGC) in the UK for such a buffer was seen as the ideal by both staff associations and university presidents.

The Commission cited numerous submissions to it which advocated, for the Irish system, a body very similar to the UGC. However, it rejected this model on various grounds. Firstly, it envisaged that its Permanent Commission would be required to deal with the whole higher education system and not just the universities. Then it envisaged a body which would be actively concerned with planning and development and not just the grant-allocating task of the UGC. Finally, it did not believe that in the Irish circumstances, such a planning and grant-giving body could be seen to operate impartially if the members were primarily drawn from the institutions depending on it; it proposed that the membership would be appointed by government and would consist of a part-time chairman and eight other part-time members, none of whom would be drawn from any of the institutions which came within its scope.[44]

Other recommendations of the Commission

The Commission made numerous other recommendations in relation to professional education and to a variety of smaller research bodies such as the Irish Folklore Commission or the Dublin Institute of Advanced Studies. In prescribing the future for professional education it adopted a traditionalist view of the place of medical and legal education and training in the universities but made proposals for the establishment of a technological authority which would take some responsibility for the training of engineers and for a National College of Agricultural and Veterinary Sciences which would take complete responsibility for education in agricultural science and veterinary medicine. It also made significant proposals for the financing of students in higher education

---

44 Commission on Higher Education, op. cit., *Report*, pp. 476–7.

through a scheme of scholarships and loans.

In retrospect, the major lacuna in the Commission's thinking was its failure to foresee the substantial developments which would take place through the establishment of the Regional Technical Colleges. As explained above, planning in this sector was taking place while the Commission was sitting but the Steering Committee on Technical Education was not established until 1966, at which time the Commission was finalising its Report. Nevertheless, developments in Britain where, at the time of publication of the Robbins Report in 1963, there were ten colleges of advanced technology with their emphasis increasingly on full-time work for diplomas in technology or for external degrees of London University, might have given some foretaste of likely developments in Ireland.[45]

The Summary Report of the Commission was published on 22 March 1967. The leader writer in *The Irish Times*, in an editorial headed *Expectans Expectavi*,[46] was critical of many of its recommendations:

> . . . the composition of the original Commission . . . evoked a genuine admiration for the qualities of the men and women concerned coupled with a faint sense of puzzlement that this particular group of people should have been assigned to this particular task. They were, in fact, given an impossible job; it is now a matter of record that although they have probably done a great deal better than many people would have been prepared to predict, some of their suggestions will have to be looked at very carefully indeed.

While praising the recommendations on the place of research in the universities and on the appointments systems it criticised the approach to structural planning and suggested that some of the statements in the Report were alarming:

> The idea of a permanent Commission for Higher Education is an excellent one—but why did the present Commission see fit deliberately to exclude members of university institutions from it? The unwieldiness of the National University's structure is a matter of history but why did the Commission recommend defederalisation so emphatically? The commanding presence, and opinions, of the last [sic] President of University College, Dublin, [Michael Tierney] cannot, perhaps, be ignored; but the overpowering danger in such a situation is . . . that the weakest, deprived

---

45 White, op. cit., pp. 55–7.
46 A phrase from Psalm 40 which might be translated as: 'I have waited patiently'.

of even an inadequate link with a national institution, will go to the wall.

The Irish Times went on to describe the creation of New Colleges as an 'extraordinary step'. It criticised severely the Commission's suggestion that if a substantial increase in funding for the universities were not obtained, it would recommend restrictions on numbers in an attempt to maintain standards. It finished by regretting that the paper was:

> ... in the unhappy position of having to criticise the Commission's proposals without being in a position to offer a workable alternative but this is a task—a continuing task—to which a great many people should now apply themselves. We shall, we imagine, be hearing more about it before long.

The *Irish Independent* gave the Report a more positive, if cautious, welcome. Its editorial writer stated that:

> With one exception, the recommendations do not seem revolutionary.... Two proposals leap immediately to the eye and raise important questions. The first of these—the setting up of New Colleges in Limerick and Dublin and possibly elsewhere—has already been opposed by several important members of the Commission who signed reservations about it. But at first sight, there does seem to be the germ of a good idea in it, if not necessarily in the exact form set out by the Commission.... A second striking proposal is the plan for financing students.... It seems to be becoming clearer every day that we will have to decide what the phrase social justice means in education at every level. If it means simply that the State should pay directly for the education of most people, then let us go ahead.

The writer of the editorial in the *Irish Press* was critical of the Commission's conclusions in relation to the Dublin colleges. He wrote:

> In the midst of all these and various other reforming recommendations there is one noticeable omission. The treatment of the Dublin situation in which both University College and Trinity receive public money for duplicating educational resources is dealt with solely as a religious issue. It is 'a matter of conscience' on which the Commission does not regard it proper to comment and the possibility of amalgamating the two institutions is not considered 'opportune'. Admittedly the Commission has been some years deliberating and may not have had the opportunity to take account of changes both within the universities and in public opinion towards them. Certainly there seem substantial grounds—educational, financial, social—for suggesting that the situation of the two Dublin colleges be

re-examined more forthrightly.

There was surprisingly little comment in the newspapers from normally eloquent academic staff members of the universities; the only significant contribution was a series of four comprehensive articles in *The Irish Times* by Garret FitzGerald. Academic opinion, however, was to become very vocal within a few weeks when the Minister for Education made his dramatic announcement on the relationship between Trinity and UCD.

Donogh O'Malley on his way into Leinster House in the 1960s. (The Irish Times)

4. The merger

A marriage has been arranged

On 18 April 1967, a month after the Commission on Higher Education's *Summary Report* rejected the idea of a merger between Trinity College, Dublin and University College, Dublin, the Minister for Education, Donogh O'Malley, in a major public speech announced his plans for just such a merger.

The Minister started his announcement by stating:

> Everybody, I think, will agree that the university situation in Dublin is far from being satisfactory. We have here in the capital city of a small country what are to all intents and purposes two separate and very differently constituted University institutions, each endowed in major part by the State, but each ploughing its own furrow with virtually no provision, formal or even informal, for coordination of their efforts or the sharing by them of what must always be scarce but very valuable national resources. Those resources comprise knowledge and skills of the highest quality, accommodation, equipment and material generally.

Mr O'Malley went on to summarise the financial commitments of the state to the Dublin university institutions and the increase to those commitments arising from the expected rise in student numbers and the building plans of the universities. He continued by restating the arguments advanced by the Commission against the proposed expansion of Trinity's student numbers at a time when such a large proportion of those students originated outside the state, but asserted:

> Let me here digress for a moment in order to state clearly and unequivocally that I am strongly in favour of a leavening of non-Irish students in our Universities. An admixture of foreign students is a healthy thing in itself and moreover is in accord with the best Irish traditions. Ever since Colmcille left Ireland for ever in 563, Irishmen have been striving, as far as circumstances permitted, to make some return of the debt they owe to the rest of the world. . . . Furthermore, we Europeans, who through the action of Providence and not, I should say, through any merits of our own, owe to ancient Palestine, ancient Greece and ancient Rome our flying start over

the rest of the human race in almost everything that matters, owe in turn to the developing countries of today, to Africa, Asia and Latin America, a sharing with them of that priceless heritage.

I favour strongly therefore our receiving a reasonable number of foreign students, but consider that it is unhealthy, both from their point of view and ours, that there should be any large block of them (and especially a large block from any country already developed) in any particular College with almost none in the others, as is the case at present. They should be more evenly distributed throughout our Colleges.

In a brief reference to the recommendations of the Commission he noted:

Now that a Summary of the Commission's Report has been issued, it emerges that it does not contain any recommendations for the establishing of a formally defined relationship between the two Colleges. . . .

For the reasons I have given, however, the Government considers that the public interest demands the establishment of a formal relationship between the two Colleges. The Government has accordingly authorised me to announce that it is their intention to proceed on the lines of my proposals of December last. Those proposals were framed on the basis of there being one University of Dublin, to contain two Colleges, each complementary to the other.

The two Colleges would be founded on the two existing institutions, University College and Trinity College. One University in Dublin would involve one University authority, statutorily established on a democratic basis, with a subsidiary authority, similarly constituted, for each of the two Colleges. In the matter of the identity of each College the feeling of the existing authorities will be given the utmost weight.

Having outlined some of his ideas on the disposition of facilities between the two colleges he went on, with his eye firmly on the likely Protestant fears:

This moment is not without its solemnity. It marks the end of an era in the long story of university education in Ireland and also, it seems to me, the history of the country itself. Each of the institutions concerned has had a remarkable past and each has played a part of the highest importance to Ireland. Trinity, the elder sister, when founded more than three and a half centuries ago, was intended to be one of a number of Colleges of the University of Dublin.[1] It is late in the day, but not too late, for it to become so.

In the intervening period it has produced a number of *alumni* whose fame

---

[1] This contention has been questioned at times—particularly by defenders of Trinity College.

has shed lustre not only on their College, but also on their country, in every part of the world—Swift (whose tercentenary, just now being celebrated, has attracted scholars from near and far), Berkeley, Goldsmith, Burke, Hamilton, to mention but a few. More important perhaps to us than even the world-wide renown of these is that in every generation since Swift, Trinity College has produced from the ranks of the ascendancy a number of champions of the oppressed majority, some of them even becoming its leaders. The names of Swift himself, of Berkeley, Burke, Grattan, Tone, Emmet, Davis, Hyde and many others are sufficient evidence of that.

There may be those who will feel, mistakenly, that under the new arrangements something of 'that which once was great has passed away'. It is to be noted also, however—there would be no point in ignoring it—that the College as an institution was for long the pillar and prop of the oppressors. This is to be noted, but not remembered. The past in that regard is past. Besides, Trinity is not going to pass away. It will be merely taking the final step across the threshold of that mansion to which it properly belongs, the Irish nation.

His comments on the much larger UCD were less effusive, perhaps, coming from a minister from the Fianna Fáil party about an institution which was still, at that time, seen as a stronghold of the opposition Fine Gael party:

> University College, too, although it is only a few years since it held its first centenary, has already carved out its special place among us. Founded by the Catholic Hierarchy in 1854 as the Catholic University of Ireland, its first Rector was the illustrious John Henry Newman, that lord of language and ideas whose lectures on 'The Idea of a University', first delivered in Dublin, are more and more studied in every University in the world. Following the Catholic University's weary 'struggle with fortune', as it was called at the time, it survived as University College under the prudent direction of the Jesuit Fathers, under whom it held its own and more than its own academically, but without State support, till 1908, when it received statutory recognition as a Constituent College of the newly established National University.
>
> In its time it has numbered among its alumni or staff those great scholars Eugene O'Curry, Father Edmund Hogan, Eoin MacNeill and Douglas Hyde, the last two joint founders of the Gaelic League and MacNeill the founder of the scientific study of our early history.
>
> Later it gave us Pearse and MacDonagh, who might be said to have stepped straight out of its portals into history. University College can claim too the name of Kevin Barry, which is graven in the hearts of the Irish people, and many other such who played a valiant part in the struggle for independence, not forgetting our present Uachtarán. Since 1916 its special function has been to give our

country the larger part of its teachers, scientists, engineers, doctors, dentists, architects, administrators and other professional experts, as well as its quota of public men, whose services have over the last fifty years been increasingly required in the building of the new Ireland.

There may be some also to deplore that it has not been seen fit to give University College the status of a separate University, such as Newman dimly foresaw. To those I would say that to form a part of the University of Dublin is a destiny which will eventually add greater prestige to University College than if it were to stand apart on its own.

Finally, and rather elliptically, the Minister referred to the religious orientation of the new university:

> ... the new University of Dublin will not be 'neutral' denominationally, but multi-denominational, with the fullest respect and recognition for all denominations of students and the fullest mutual respect among them for each other. 'Neutralism' in relation to what happened two thousand years ago in Palestine would not have been and is not a concept that would have any appeal for the vast majority of Irish parents, whatever their denomination. In the future University of Dublin there will be provision for both Catholic and Protestant Schools of Divinity or Theology. This was not permissible for University College under the 1908 Act.

He closed his statement by expressing his optimism that this 'national problem' would finally be solved satisfactorily, with good will.

The immediate response to the Minister's announcement of what quickly came to be referred to as 'the merger', was one of alarm. The *Irish Independent* produced two separate editorials on the topic on the following day. In the first of these, the writer exclaimed 'The extraordinary university eruption of yesterday is enough to leave a prudent man speechless.' Despite this assertion the writer continued:

> ... a few words may be found to raise some practical questions about the Government's decision on the future of our universities. The attitude of the Catholic community and in particular the bishops, towards the promised shape of higher education is, of course, of critical importance.

The writer went on to question the Minister's assertions on the savings to be expected from the merger and pointed out that the real problem facing university education was the expected large increase in student numbers rather than some duplication between the facilities available in TCD and UCD. The editorial then went on to praise the Commission for having proposed novel solutions to the problems of expansion—presumably referring to the New Colleges proposal—and raised the question of there being an optimum size for a single university. Finally, it suggested that there was a need to think more deeply about 'the flood that seems to be rising before us.'[2]

The writer of the second editorial was more approving of the Minister:

> Rarely has a nettle been so firmly grasped. In one half-hour Mr O'Malley presumed to render irrelevant the accumulated arguments of a century over Catholic attendance at Trinity College. For, in the Minister's scheme of things as we read him, the kind of Trinity to which the ban applied will be no more. Which is not to say that the argument has ended. The proclaiming of a multi-denominational university can be taken as a fair statement of intent. But its realisation lies outside the Minister's competence. It cannot be given life without the approval of the denominations, as the ghost of Sir Robert Peel could tell O'Malley.[3] The deliberate refusal of the Minister to undertake prior consultation may therefore prove, with hindsight, to have been extremely hazardous.

The editorial continued with words of encouragement for the Minister:

> The Bishops will undoubtedly need assurances about the character of the new university before they give it their blessing. Here it may be that Mr O'Malley is on strong ground. A multi-denominational institution would, in fact, be an advance upon the existing National University of Ireland, hampered by its want of Theology faculties and its "neutral" charter.[4] The provision of full facilities for the denominations would give religion elbow-room to expand and become an active force in university life.[5]

An *Irish Press* editorial also used the 'grasping the nettle' metaphor in giving a guarded welcome to the Minister's proposal but it continued:

---

2 *Irish Independent* 19 April 1967.

3 Robert Peel had established the Queen's University and its colleges in the 1840s.

4 It was the 1908 Universities Act rather than the charter of the NUI which prescribed that no test of religious belief could be imposed on any person as a condition of becoming or continuing to be a professor, lecturer, fellow, scholar or student of the university; at that time the concept of a non-denominational or a multi-denominational Faculty of Theology was not envisaged.

5 *Irish Independent* 19 April 1967.

The effect of rationalisation on staff-student ratios is apparent but its benefits to the great mass of school-leavers currently excluded from the relatively few who gain access to universities is less evident. And the issue of preserving established traditions within the existing colleges is easier to raise than to meet.[6]

In *The Irish Times*, a front-page headline proclaimed: 'O'Malley announces wedding plans' and its editorial was headed 'Mixed Marriage'. The editorial writer was more positive towards the proposals than his counterparts in the other Dublin papers and claimed that 'Some form of close association between UCD and TCD has for so long appeared not only rational, but necessary, that Mr O'Malley's sudden move should have had an air of inevitability.' The Minister's statement was described as 'highly colourful, emotional, and historically perhaps a little naïf—from Columcille to Burke, from patronising to threatening, from blunt statement to poetic flight—it was very much Mr O'Malley, bluff, guileful but, in this case effective.'[7] The writer went on to praise the Minister's decision not to consult the hierarchy before his announcement, to opt for a new federal arrangement rather than a complete unification and to emphasise the need for improvement in the staff-student ratios of the institutions. The writer continued:

> We are on the verge of a national debate which will rival any we have seen in previous years not only in scope but in vehemence. The protagonists will be among the most vocal and eloquent people in the country, both academic and clerical. The university world will be thrown open to inspection and examination as it has not been for half a century.[8]

In a brief discussion on the Minister's proposals in Dáil Éireann on the following day, he informed the deputies that the government had come to a decision 'in principle' that there would be a University

---

6 *Irish Press*, 19 April 1967.

7 Mr O'Malley had a reputation as a dynamic and colourful, if somewhat buccaneering, political animal. In particular, his announcement of the scheme for free secondary education in September 1966, which was widely believed to have been made before there had been any cabinet discussion of the issue, gave credence to this view of his character. Seán O'Connor, who was the Assistant Secretary in the Department of Education responsible for secondary education, has given an interesting account of this episode in his memoir: *A Troubled Sky*, (1986) Dublin, Educational Research Centre, St Patrick's College, pp. 141-6.

8 *The Irish Times* 19 April 1967.

of Dublin, with a common board or authority and two colleges. He assured them that the views of the interests concerned with regard to all other questions would be obtained before the government made a decision on all other matters.[9]

The national newspapers reported the reaction of various individuals and groups to the minister's announcement of the merger over the next few days. The Provost of Trinity, Dr McConnell, in a brief personal statement said that 'for a good many years now my college has expressed its desire for close cooperation with other university institutions in this country with the object of ensuring the highest standards of Irish university education and of avoiding unnecessary duplication. I can, therefore, say with some confidence that Trinity College will look at the Minister's plans with the utmost sympathy.' He went on to express his anxiety that:

> ... the good and great traditions of Trinity College and of the University of Dublin will continue. These are old and honoured institutions of worldwide renown and I am very glad to see that the Minister proposes that they shall be preserved. We shall understand the equal concern of our sister college to preserve her valued traditions.... I can say personally how much I would look forward to cooperating with our friends in University College and with the Minister in making a success of this new and exciting development of the University of Dublin.[10]

The Governing Body of UCD, in a statement which was as interesting for the speed with which it was produced as for its content, stated that its members agreed with the Minister:

> ... that the existence of two teaching universities in Dublin was the cause of much wasteful duplication.... It is our opinion, however, that the benefits sought by the Minister would be best achieved by a complete unification of the two institutions. We consider that the time has come when the Dublin University question, now more than a century old, should be finally settled by the founding of a new University of Dublin, which would pool all resources, intellectual, material and financial under a single authority.[11]

---

9 Dáil Debates, 20 April 1967, Vol. 227, Col. 2193. In the discussion, Michael O'Leary (Labour) asked the Minister what he would do in future with the Chancellor of the NUI. The Minister declined to answer. The Chancellor was Éamon de Valera who had been elected to the office in 1922 and who was, at that time, the President of Ireland.
10 *Irish Independent* 19 April 1967.
11 Ibid.

The Irish Times reported a Fine Gael statement which claimed that the Minister's plans had been a response to its own proposals issued some months previously. Fine Gael expressed its concern that 'minority interests' would be safeguarded. *The Irish Times* also reported a statement from the leader of the Labour party, Brendan Corish, welcoming the merger proposal and, the following day, published a statement from Cardinal Conway[12] in which he said that his initial reaction was that 'the plan contained a number of good ideas and that it could mark a positive step towards a rationalisation of the situation in all its aspects.'[13] Archbishop McQuaid did not wish to make any comment.

The *Irish Independent* had canvassed the views of a number of present and former academic staff of the Dublin university institutions on the proposals. The former UCD President, Dr Michael Tierney, rather oddly welcomed the government's announcement (which he appeared not to have understood) saying that he hoped it meant that 'UCD and TCD would be united as one great institution and not as two colleges in a new University of Dublin.... It was best to relegate to history institutions which had their roots in an unfortunate past and to begin to plan on ground free of all historical encumbrances for a better future.'[14]

Professor Dudley Edwards from the UCD history department, queried why the Minister had favoured the maintenance of two separate colleges in Dublin and had not opted for complete integration. The Trinity historian, Professor T. W. Moody[15] who had been a member of the Commission on Higher Education, was quoted as saying that 'The Merger was very much to be desired.' David Thornley[16] from Trinity also welcomed the merger announcement while Senator Owen Sheehy Skeffington,[17] also from Trinity, commented that the unifica-

---

12 Cardinal William Conway was Archbishop of Armagh, and thus titular head of the Irish hierarchy, from 1958 to 1977.

13 *The Irish Times* 22 April 1967.

14 *Irish Independent* 19 April 1967.

15 (1907-1984)

16 David Thornley was at that time the Honorary Secretary of the Irish Federation of University Teachers (IFUT) which was to play an active part in subsequent debates on the merger.

17 Dr Sheehy Skeffington's father had been the first Registrar of UCD after 1908;

tion of Trinity and UCD might run into a lot of 'secret opposition from a variety of sources'.[18] Finally, the President of the Ulster Liberal Association was quoted as stating that if Trinity could maintain its traditional freedom he welcomed amalgamation and continued: 'I don't think there will be any fewer Northern Protestants wanting to go to Trinity because what attracts them is Trinity's tradition, its status and above all its freedom.'[19]

The first published letter on the merger in the national newspapers was from Joe Foyle, a well-known conservative Catholic commentator on matters political, religious and educational. He welcomed the merger but expressed concern for the future of Protestantism in Trinity because of the sheer weight of numbers of Catholics. He also adverted to the 'mixed marriage dangers'. Trinity, he thought, should:

> ... concentrate on being a humanities institution of higher education for Protestants, while sharing professional/technological education facilities elsewhere with Catholics. This arrangement ... would minimise the mixed-marriages danger since Catholics and Protestants would be studying together only in faculties where the proportion of female students would be very small.[20]

Trinity vs UCD: A truceless Cold War

To understand fully the public reaction to the merger announcement, it is necessary to look again at the contrasting natures of Trinity and UCD and the role they played in the Ireland of the 1960s. Ireland at that time was beginning to emerge from decades of economic decline and massive emigration; the Census of 1971 would show a halt to the decrease in population which had started in 1841. The commemoration in 1966 of the 50th anniversary of the Rising of 1916, appeared to show that the establishment of the 26-county Republic of Ireland in 1922 was now a cause for celebration rather than a stimulus for resentful nationalism.

Religion was still a dominant force in Irish life although, in the aftermath of the Second Vatican Council, the tone of the interventions of

he was murdered during the 1916 Rising.
18 *Irish Independent* 20 April 1967.
19 Ibid.
20 *The Irish Times* 21 April 21 1967

the Catholic voice in public affairs had begun to change. Dr McQuaid was to remain Archbishop of Dublin until 1972 but his role in the consciousness of the Irish people had been weakened by the liberal trends licensed by post-conciliar thinking in the Church. A new, informed, lay Catholic voice began to be heard in public debate replacing fundamentalist movements such as the defunct Maria Duce[21] organisation. The Catholic hierarchy no longer had a monopoly on the representation of Catholic views on political and social affairs.

The Protestant population of the Republic of Ireland continued a decline in numbers which had been evident since the early years of the century. It had represented about 8 per cent of the population at the time of independence in 1922. By the time of the 1961 Census that figure had fallen to less than 5 per cent. Although there was an urban working-class element in that population, Protestants were commonly perceived to be members of the middle or upper classes and to have retained an Anglo-Irish identity. As recently as 1957, the Fethard-on-Sea boycott of Protestant businesses in the Co. Wexford town had demonstrated that Protestant-Catholic relationships could still be a source of communal tension.[22]

In 1960 there were still Protestant hospitals, Protestant banks, Protestant golf clubs and Protestant businesses in Ireland, particularly in the Dublin region. *The Irish Times* was the Protestant newspaper, although it was to begin its evolution into a national institution and into the paper of record for Ireland later in the decade. The jewel in the crown of the Protestant community in Ireland was Trinity College Dublin with its distinguished history, its world-wide reputation and its impressive buildings in the heart of the capital city.

---

21 Maria Duce was an extreme Catholic group which produced a magazine, *Fiat*, with a considerable circulation. It was both anti-Protestant and anti-semitic in its views. It functioned in the 1940s and 50s but was dissolved by the Catholic Church in 1955.

22 In Fethard-on-Sea, the local Catholic clergy had called for a boycott of Protestant businesses in the town in response to the Protestant partner in a mixed marriage fleeing the country with her children to avoid having to send them to the local Catholic school. The resulting boycott, which gained widespread publicity, was finally ended when it was condemned by the then Taoiseach, Éamon de Valera.

TCD in the 1960s

The extent to which the student body of Trinity was Protestant in the middle of the 20th century and some of the reasons for this characteristic, have been discussed in Chapter 2. Table 2.4 showed that in 1950, 51 per cent of the student body were Anglican and 22 per cent Catholic. No data have been published for later years but there is no reason to believe that the figures had changed substantially in the following decade despite an increasing focus, notably by the Archbishop of Dublin, on the Church ban on the attendance of Catholics there.

Table 2.3 shows that in the 1965/6 session, 28.3 per cent of the student body in Trinity came from Great Britain and 23.3 per cent came from Northern Ireland of which a significant proportion was Catholic. The Commission on Higher Education had expressed its concern at these figures in that they signified a financial subsidy being applied to students from another developed jurisdiction. In terms of the common perception of Trinity among the Irish population as a whole, this large group of students from the UK added to the 'foreign-ness' of the college. A recently published collection of memoirs from people who were students in Trinity in the 1960s gives some interesting insights on this matter.[23] Nicholas Grene writes that 'Trinity in [1961–5] was still dominated by English students. . . . With their public-school accents, their superior sophistication, the resented belief that they came to Trinity for purely snobbish reasons as Oxbridge rejects, they were envied and disliked by Irish students in about equal parts.'[24]

Another ex-student writes that 'Trinity in those days had a high percentage of Oxbridge rejects and ex-public school pupils. . . . The [UK] government financed us; my fees were paid. So was my board and lodging'.[25] Roy Foster, one of the very few contributors who appear to have been aware of the propinquity of UCD, notes that 'In 1967, Trinity's relation to its immediate surroundings was still faintly

23 Sebastian Balfour et al. (Eds). (2009) *Trinity Tales: Trinity College Dublin in the Sixties* Dublin, The Lilliput Press.
24 Ibid. p 271. Nicholas Grene is Professor of English Literature in TCD. From an Irish Protestant background, he was a student in Trinity from 1965 to 1969.
25 Ibid., p. 185. Anne Heyno is an English journalist and academic who was a Trinity student from 1962 to 1966. At that time, English local authorities which administered the relatively generous grants for English university students, treated students attending Trinity on the same basis as students attending UK universities.

exotic.'[26] Another contributor refers to Trinity as 'an Irish Tangier'.[27]

Data on the religious affiliation of the staff of Trinity College were published by Dr Alfred O'Rahilly, former president of UCC, in *Studies* in 1961.[28] In an article supporting the Catholic ban on attendance at Trinity he cited a figure of three Catholic professors compared to 40 Protestant professors and 21 Catholic lecturers compared to 102 Protestant lecturers.[29] He noted further that all the important officers and all but two members of the board and all 18 tutors were Protestant.

Additional information on the religious affiliation of Trinity staff and students was supplied in a statement issued by the board of Trinity College in March 1967.[30] This statement was prepared in order to demonstrate Trinity's willingness to accept Catholic members and to place the blame for its distorted profile on the Catholic authorities. The statement indicated that at that time 27 per cent of the academic staff and 24 per cent of the student body were Catholic. Further, 13 per cent of the Fellows were Catholic as were 37 per cent of the tutors.

No data on the country of origin of the academic staff of the university is available. However, an analysis of the Dublin University Calendar for 1966/7 gives some indication of the orientation of the academic staff showing the location of the universities where either their primary or higher degrees were obtained. A comparison is shown in Table 4.1 of these data with similar data for UCD in the same year. While the data show that, in both institutions, the great majority of staff were graduates of the universities in which they were working. more than one third of the Trinity staff held degrees, either primary or higher, from UK universities while only 8 per cent of the UCD staff had similar qualifications.

---

26 Ibid. p. 234. Roy Foster is the Carroll Professor of Irish History at the University of Oxford. He was a student in Trinity from 1967 to 1971.

27 Ibid., p. 49. Damien Duggan-Ryan was a student in Trinity from 1960 to 1964.

28 Alfred O'Rahilly. 'The Irish University Question' *Studies*, Vol. 50 p. 249 (Autumn 1961).

29 O'Rahilly, who had been ordained as a Catholic priest following his retirement from the presidency of UCC in 1954, was a commentator in the same mould as Michael Tierney in UCD. Some of the background to the work of gathering these figures is given by McCartney (op. cit., p. 211).

30 Trinity College Board Register: Companion Volume p. 73 TCD archives, MUN/V/6/12.

Table 4.1 Numbers of academic staff with degrees from universities other than their own

Degree-granting university	Trinity	UCD
Trinity	–	2
NUI	37	–
Oxbridge	45	21
Other UK	68	9
Other European	5	15
US	11	12
Total staff numbers	338	374

Source: Calendars of UCD and Trinity for 1966/7. The figures were obtained by counting those who had recorded either primary or higher degrees from universities other than the one where they were working. In cases where there were two other universities noted, the one associated with the higher of the two degrees was recorded. The NUI degrees do not distinguish between the colleges of the NUI at which the person was studying. Of the 37 members of the Trinity staff with NUI qualifications, 86 per cent were teaching in professional schools—particularly the medical school—in Trinity.

UCD in the 1960s

In marked contrast to Trinity, UCD, at the time of the announcement of the merger was a predominantly Catholic, 26-county Irish, university. McCartney gives a detailed picture of the relationship between the college and the Catholic Church; he reports that 97 per cent of the student body was Catholic in 1960.[31] And this was not a mere nominal allegiance as it perhaps has become later; daily Mass-going was common and in the libraries students routinely stood for the Angelus at mid-day. The figure would not have changed significantly by 1967 although the allegiance of the students to the dictates of the hierarchy might, perhaps, have diminished in the aftermath of the Vatican Council. No data on the religious affiliation of the staff members has been published although Michael Tierney mischievously claimed at one point that UCD had more Protestant staff members than Trinity had Catholic ones.

The geographical origins of students at UCD were, also, quite different from those in Trinity. Table 4.2 shows that more than 91 per cent of UCD students in the 1966/7 session had their domicile in the Republic of Ireland and almost 95 per cent were from Ireland, North and South, while the comparable figures for Trinity were 41 per cent and 66 per cent respectively.

31 McCartney op. cit., pp. 159–226.

Table 4.2 Domicile of full-time students at UCD in the 1966/7 session.

Student domicile	Numbers	Percentage
Dublin City & County	3,704	50.3
Rest of Leinster	1,212	16.4
Munster	992	13.5
Connaught	503	6.8
Ulster (Rep. of I.)	327	4.4
Ulster (Northern I.)	251	3.4
Great Britain	144	2.0
Other	237	3.2
Total	7,370	100

Source: UCD: *Report of the President for 1966/7*

UCD at that time saw itself as being the real 'national' university and would have accepted with pride the words of Donogh O'Malley in his merger statement in which he described UCD's function as being 'to give our country the larger part of its teachers, scientists, engineers, doctors, dentists, architects, administrators and other professional experts, as well as its quota of public men, whose services have over the last fifty years been increasingly required in the building of the new Ireland.'

As an example of this role, he might have cited the membership of the Supreme Court in 1967, in which five of the six sitting members were former UCD students while the one Protestant member was a former Trinity student.[32]

Relationships between UCD and Trinity

The relationship between Trinity and UCD at the time of the announcement of the merger in 1967 might charitably be described as distant. A typical Irish Catholic view of those relationships was given by the then President of UCD, Michael Tierney, in his written evidence to the Commission on Higher Education.[33] In describing the relationship between TCD and UCD as a 'truceless cold war' he criticised 'the use of the name of Dublin by a minority institution with its peculiar history and background [as] definitely injurious to the institution established for and frequented by the vast majority of

---

[32] It was the invariable practice that one member of the Supreme Court would be a Protestant; this member would inevitably be a Trinity graduate.

[33] Tierney Memorandum No. 1. pp. 4–14, TCD archives, Box 7150-3,

Irish students.' He stated that the 'revenues of Trinity College were largely drawn from the confiscated lands of Irish Catholic "rebels"' but nevertheless claimed that no-one 'in University College has any wish to be hostile to Trinity College' and that there 'would be no objection to a fair provision by way of endowment for Trinity College as a Protestant institution drawing a large proportion of its students from abroad.'

Dr Tierney claimed that the position of Trinity College was harmful to UCD and that 'the persistence of Trinity College in holding itself out as a suitable university for Catholics and therefore as a rival to University College had resulted 'in a pressure to lower standards, a dissipation of limited resources and an unseemly scramble for an impossible equality of treatment at many different levels.' He continued: 'it now very frequently happens that students of University College, whose achievement at their primary degree in their own College does not entitle them to proceed for higher degrees in their own College, are eagerly accepted for such degrees in Trinity College.' He finally complained that:

> ... in recent propaganda directed towards people of Irish descent in the United States, claims for financial assistance have been based on the alleged 'national' character of Trinity College. In more recent efforts to obtain funds in Great Britain, what has been stressed is Trinity's quality as an outpost of British culture and religion '*in partibus infidelium*', while at the same time some of the greatest treasures of early Irish art, acquired by Trinity College during the wreck of our native institutions, have been exhibited in London for the benefit of this Janus-headed University.[34]

The Provost of Trinity, Dr McConnell, in oral evidence to the Commission, understandably rejected many of the views put forward by Michael Tierney and the role suggested for the college by him as an enclave for Protestants. He described the relations between Trinity and UCD as follows:

> My experience is that the relations between most of the departments in University College, Dublin and in Trinity College are very good; between the staffs of a good many of the departments of the two colleges, the relations are excellent. ... the relations between the mathematics departments

---

34 Ibid. While some of Dr Tierney's colleagues in UCD might have baulked at the language used by him in reference to Trinity, the Governing Body had given him *carte blanche* to speak on behalf of the college

in University College and Trinity College are excellent and could not be better.³⁵ I think that the same is true of a great many of the departments and faculties—most of them, I would say. And I think that the relations between the students in University College and in Trinity College are good at present, as far as I can judge. Unfortunately, and much to my regret, the relations are not nearly as good at the top – at the administration level.³⁶

In a separate written submission to the Commission, the Board of Trinity College was less whole-hearted than the Provost on the question of relationships with UCD stating that the Board was 'willing to proceed as far as may be possible' towards co-operation with UCD and that '[one] form of co-operation would be in the planning of new developments or departments to avoid overlapping. The College has already adopted this policy in some recent developments.'³⁷ The developments referred to were in the areas of engineering and agriculture.

While it is impossible to determine, in any precise way, the quality of relations between the two colleges at that time, one potential source of data is the information published annually in the Report of the President of UCD on the academic activities of the academic staff of the college.³⁸ In the report for 1966/7, in a listing of 290 publications by UCD academic staff, only two publications show joint authorship between staff of UCD and Trinity. These publications were in the areas of history and of public health. ³⁹ A further 50 pages in the Report listing the diverse activities of academic departments and their staff during the year show just one lecture being given by a UCD staff member to Trinity students, one lecture by a Trinity staff member to UCD students, one talk by a UCD staff member to a Trinity student society and one talk by a Trinity staff member to a UCD student society. In addition, three UCD staff members are shown as acting as

---

35 McConnell was a mathematician.
36 Commission on Higher Education, op. cit., *Report*, p. 437.
37 Ibid., p. 434.
38 University College Dublin *Report of the President for 1966/7*.
39 A number of UCD historians were involved in the series 'A Course of Irish History' jointly edited by Professor Moody from Trinity and Professor F. X. Martin from UCD. Geoffrey Bourke from the Department of Public Health in UCD published a paper jointly with J. A. Coughlan from the Medical Research Council of Ireland, which was located in Trinity College.

external examiners in Trinity.[40] These limited data appear to cast some considerable doubt on the sanguine view of the Provost regarding relations between the colleges.

Whatever about relations between the staff in the two colleges, relationships between the student bodies at Trinity and UCD at the time were, despite the cautious optimism of the provost, almost non-existent. The views of Trinity students expressed in *Trinity Tales*,[41] quoted above, indicate that many of them were hardly aware that they were studying in Ireland, let alone living a short distance away from a sister university college. There was certainly a similar lack of concern among UCD students about the student body on the other side of Stephen's Green. It was only in the sporting arena that any regular contact took place between the two groups but these contests did as much to emphasise the differences between the groups as to reduce them. The annual 'Colours match' between the rugby teams of the two colleges was the high point of this sporting connection. The listing of the team members with details of the secondary schools attended, which were usually published in the Irish newspapers of the time, served to emphasise the different backgrounds of the two student groups. The *Irish Independent* gave the details for the Colours match of 1966/7 showing that the team from UCD had three members from each of St Mary's and Castleknock, two from Gonzaga and one each from Blackrock, Rockwell, Glenstal, Clongowes, Newbridge, CUS and Terenure. The Trinity team, by contrast, had one member each from High School, Mountjoy, Wesley, Middleton Grammar, Sligo Grammar, Belfast Royal Academy, Campbell College, Coleraine Academical and Magee in Ireland and Hurstpierpoint, Cowbridge Grammar, St Edward's in Oxford, Brentwood, Douai and Belmont Abbey in Great Britain (the last two being, of course, Catholic schools).[42] These lists provide a graphic illustration of the cultural divide between the student bodies of the two university institutions.

The announcement by the Minister for Education on 18 April was seen

---

40 Professor James Tierney (Classics), Dr Roger McHugh (English) and Dr Louis Roche (French) acted as external examiners in Trinity in 1966/7.
41 Balfour et al., op. cit.
42 *Irish Independent* 30 November 1966

by him as the ending of a lengthy, contentious episode in Irish history. Given the dissimilarities between the two university institutions outlined above and the hostility expressed by the former President of UCD towards Trinity, the initial public welcome for a merger between the two rival institutions must have given him grounds for optimism that his plans would be realised without undue delay. Rather than an ending, however, his merger proposals heralded the beginning of a decade of debate, controversy and argument during which the two universities did, at last, come together but only to defeat the Minister's plans. Sadly, Donogh O'Malley died within a few months of his announcement.

5. Discussion and dissension

Reaction in Trinity to the merger proposal

The Board of Trinity College, in its first cautious response to the Minister's announcement, issued a public statement which said that 'The decision of the Government to ensure the continuity of the traditions of scholarship associated with the names of Trinity College and of University College must be in the best interests of both institutions and higher education in Ireland.' The statement went on to express the hope that discussions to establish the best means of achieving these objectives would begin without delay. It continued:

> Trinity College has developed strong links throughout Ireland and across the world over its long history. The Board of the College recognises that these links must continue to contribute to the development of Dublin's university tradition. The strength of the College's best tradition in scholarship springs from independence of thought and freedom of expression. It is essential that these freedoms will continue to flourish within the University of Dublin and its Colleges.[1]

This reference to 'independence of thought and freedom of expression' was to be a recurring theme in statements on the proposed merger coming from within Trinity. This is partly a coded reference to the need to protect the position of Protestantism in an overwhelmingly Catholic Ireland. But it also reflects a feeling that such freedoms were not current in UCD under the presidency of Michael Tierney and his successor and that Archbishop McQuaid exercised an undue influence in the affairs of that college. In Trinity, Archbishop McQuaid was seen as the embodiment of an obscurantist Catholicism which, *inter alia*, prevented Catholics from attending as students there.

And in the background there was a shift of feeling in the majority Catholic community, a feeling that a new, more liberal, Catholic constituency (the *Irish Times* audience) was emerging post Vatican II.

1 Ibid., 78/3.

The Board's statement was made in the light of the instantaneous response from the UCD Governing Body which, as noted previously, called for the complete unification of the two Dublin colleges. Trinity, therefore, was on the defensive, with the threat of absorption by the much larger institution in Earlsfort Terrace now on the agenda and with no defence organisations likely to spring into being, as had happened, as we have seen, in response to the report of the Fry Commission in 1907.

At the meeting on 10 May, the Board noted the first organised response to the merger proposals from staff within the college. On 3 May the junior Fellows had passed a resolution which urged the Board to ask departments in the college to consider internally what cooperation was possible with UCD.[2] The resolution went on to ask the Board to work out the irreducible requirements for maintaining the traditions of TCD. The Board welcomed this approach and decided that representatives of the junior Fellows should discuss with the Fellows 'the requirements which, in the Board's opinion, were essential to ensure the maintenance of the best traditions in scholarship, hitherto associated with the name of Trinity College'.[3]

This early involvement of a grouping of the academic staff of the college in the deliberations of the Board was to be a feature of future activities of the Board and Trinity. It was characteristic of the attitudes to authority within the college that such democratic manifestations were seen as appropriate. Undoubtedly, also, it was seen by the Board that the support of the whole Trinity community would be vital in the defence of the 'traditions and freedoms' of the college. The involvement of the staff in this way was to lead to changes in the way in which staff were organised in the college.

Attitudes in UCD were quite different. Although Michael Tierney had retired from the presidency some years earlier, his autocratic style of management persisted. Academic staff involvement in the deliberations of the Governing Body of the college was not encouraged. During the debates of the next decade in response to the merger proposals, therefore, the voice of staff organisations in UCD was constantly heard in counterpoint to the statements of the President and

2 TCD Board Register, 83/8 TCD archives, MUN/V/5/34.
3 Ibid.

Governing Body.

The Minister now invited the governing authorities of both colleges to meet him; UCD met with him on 1 June and he planned to meet with Trinity on 7 June. On 6 June, the day before this meeting, a statement was issued by the Fellows. It noted that after seven weeks, it was time to put on record what the Fellows of Trinity College understood by the Minister's assurance that he wished to maintain the identity of Trinity. They stated:

> Trinity College is one of the oldest universities [in the world] of the campus type. The continued identity of Trinity College means that this community aspect of university education will be at least as strongly present in the TCD of the proposed new university as it is today.
>
> It is our determination to preserve, along with a wide spread of subjects and courses, the freedom of teaching and discussion which both the academic staff and the students enjoy in Trinity College at present.
>
> We believe that close cooperation and association between Trinity College and University College can achieve valuable improvements in teaching and in research facilities that each now offers. We affirm our wish to continue to explore the most useful form of this cooperation.

The minutes of the Board meeting of 7 June record details of the meeting which had taken place with the Minister that morning.[4] He had presented a prepared text, which had also been presented to the UCD Governing Body the previous week. Initially, the Minister dismissed the UCD proposal for a 'total assimilation' of the two colleges and stated that his plan for a university with two colleges had been 'decided firmly' by the government. He then put forward a number of concrete ideas to flesh out the skeletal structures contained in the 18 April statement. Among the ideas proposed by him were that:

- The university governing authority would be made up of equal numbers from each of the colleges with a corresponding number of state appointees; perhaps in the ratio of 7:7:7 or 10:10:10.
- The university would own the existing campuses and the present property and equipment of the colleges. It would appoint the staff members and allocate them to one or other of the colleges.
- The university would decide in which college particular faculties might be located, in which college particular subjects or

---

4 TCD Board Register, 7 June 1967, TCD archives, MUN/V/5/34.

courses would be taught and in which college particular buildings might be erected.
- Faculties would be faculties of the university.
- Government grants would be paid to the university.
- There would be no division of students into colleges on a denominational basis but there would be no legal bar to the official provision of a faculty or faculties of theology or divinity in either college.
- There would be an overall national figure of, perhaps, 10 per cent admissions of non-Irish students spread evenly, as far as possible over all four Irish university institutions.
- Each college would have a spread of disciplines.

A key point in the Minister's presentation was his first suggestion with regard to a possible division of faculties between the colleges. He noted:

> One great problem will be the location of faculties. The fact that this must be governed to a great extent by the accommodation available would, at first sight, point to the smaller or professional Faculties, say Medicine, Dentistry, Veterinary Science, Law, Architecture, Commerce, Business Management, Agriculture and the like being assigned to Trinity with the larger Faculties of Arts and Science going to UCD.

It may be noted that, in a sense, the faculties of Veterinary Medicine and of Dentistry were a key to the whole merger debate as far as government disquiet about duplication and rationalisation was concerned. In Veterinary Medicine, both Trinity and UCD had complete faculties offering five-year degrees with each faculty employing its own academic staff. UCD accepted 50 students per year while Trinity accepted 10. The two faculties shared the same accommodation in the Veterinary College—a facility which was owned and maintained by the government Department of Agriculture in Shelbourne Road. In Dentistry, there were three complete, separate, faculties in Dublin—in Trinity, UCD and the Royal College of Surgeons—each offering five- or six-year degree programmes and each sharing the same facilities in the Dublin Dental Hospital. The student numbers admitted each year were: UCD—25; TCD—6; RCSI—15. Such duplication of expensive resources was an obvious irritant to government.

The Minister finally asked the Board members to prepare

memoranda on their thoughts on the desirable form of constitution for the new University of Dublin and on how they thought the merging of the two colleges might best be effected.[5]

The Provost informed the Board, that in response to the Minister's presentation, he had assured him that the Board had, from the beginning, approached the task of developing the new relationship with University College within the new University of Dublin with the greatest sympathy and understanding. He believed that the best results would come from arrangements worked out between the two colleges. The Minister had stated that he would accept an agreement of this kind which met his basic objectives.[6]

It was reported to the Board that the classicist Professor Stanford, a member of the Board and, at that time, one of the Trinity representatives in Seanad Éireann, had told the Minister that any proposal to concentrate arts and science in University College while the professional schools and social science were concentrated in Trinity would be most undesirable, as much in the interests of students as of staff.[7] This stance, which was strongly supported by the Board members, was to become the major focus of discussion and dissension between the colleges over the next few years.

At its next meeting on 21 June, the Board noted a resolution from the (Protestant) Irish Schoolmasters Association expressing alarm at reports that Irish would become compulsory for matriculation to the new university. It also considered a statement issued by IFUT which had been formulated at its annual general meeting and which asked that:

> ... the authorities in the various colleges should take the soonest possible steps to initiate discussions with their academic staffs and with each other, about the future of Higher Education in Ireland in the context of the Report of the Commission on Higher Education and the proposals of the Minister for Education for a new University in Dublin.[8]

Over the summer of 1967, opposition within Trinity to the attitude of the Minister and of the UCD Governing Body grew. On 11 July,

5 Ibid.
6 Ibid.
7 Ibid.
8 TCD Board Register, 21 June 1967, TCD archives, MUN/V/5/34.

a submission was made to the Board by the non-Fellow professors. It stated that they were unhappy about the government's decision to merge Trinity and UCD into one University of Dublin and did not welcome this proposal. They favoured the proposals made by the Commission on Higher Education and made a number of other points:

- There must be strong colleges and a strong university but in separate, defined, spheres.
- The colleges must be free to continue in their separate educational traditions.
- It is essential that the colleges should [each] form a community of students and staff from a whole range of academic disciplines living, eating, working and playing together.
- Trinity should expand to 5,000 or 6,000 students and UCD should be restricted to 8,000 students.
- The Governing Body of the University should be structured with ten representatives each from Trinity and UCD, with only three members appointed from the outside.
- The Colleges should have no outside members on their Governing Bodies.[9]
- There must be no barriers in either College to full freedom of thought and expression. All members of the academic staff must have full security of tenure, with freedom to express their views and opinions.[10]

This expression of strong opposition to the merger idea was typical of the views which were hardening within the college. The memorandum of the Board now sent to the Minister, representing the members' current negotiating position, was much stronger in defence of the status quo than their initial responses had been. In this memorandum they opened by expressing their impatience that, three months after the Minister's announcement, no meeting had taken place with UCD. They stated that they must reluctantly accept the merger because of the failure of the government to provide resources for more than 3,000

---

9 The admission of outside members, i.e. members appointed by the government, to the Board was and remained a key issue for Trinity; UCD had learned to live with such members since 1908.

10 TCD Board Register Companion Volume, p. 108 TCD archives, MUN/V/6/12.

students; this number was too small to provide the range of resources for a viable modern university. However, they insisted that they would not accept a situation in which Trinity College became merely a name within the larger university unit. They then made a number of specific points replying to suggestions from the Minister at his meeting with the Board in June:

- The proposal to move all arts and science to Belfield was 'ludicrous'. The Trinity Library and its copyright status were crucial and must be tied to education in arts.
- It was necessary to link science departments with relevant professional schools.
- Students, having matriculated, must be free to choose which college to enter, assuming that there were places available. Students from Northern Ireland, particularly, would react unfavourably to a situation in which they might be arbitrarily allocated to one college or the other by the university authority.
- It would be necessary to have some equalisation of student numbers in the two colleges, otherwise the smaller college would be 'swamped'.
- The heads of the colleges must rotate as vice-chancellor of the university.
- The governing body of the university should be composed of either nine members each from the colleges and five from outside or seven members from the colleges with three from outside.
- The differences between the colleges must be preserved. In particular, Trinity must be allowed to keep its fellowship system, although fellowship should be made open to women.[11]
- There must be no take-over of college property.[12]

11 Admission to fellowship of Trinity had, since its foundation, been confined to males. In February 1967, the board had sought legal opinion on a proposal to open fellowship to women equally with men. The opinion was favourable and the board then voted, 13 to 1, to admit women to fellowship at its meeting on 4 October. The first woman admitted to fellowship, the following year, was Professor A. J. Otway-Ruthven, the holder of the Lecky Chair in Medieval History. Sixty years earlier, the 1908 Universities Act had laid down that in the NUI colleges, women should be eligible equally with men to hold all offices.

12 TCD Board Registers Companion Volume, p. 110/111, TCD archives, MUN/V/6/12.

Reaction in UCD to the merger proposals

In contrast to the Board of Trinity, the Governing Body of UCD met infrequently—about six times each year. By chance, an extraordinary meeting had been long scheduled for 18 April, the day the Minister made his merger announcement. The main business scheduled was a consideration of the initial report of the Commission on Higher Education which had been published a month earlier. The governing body was, therefore, accidentally in a position to issue a detailed response to the Minister's proposal within a few hours of its publication.[13]

The President of UCD at this time was Dr Jeremiah Hogan, the registrar of the college under his predecessor, Michael Tierney, and a former professor of English. He had succeeded Dr Tierney in 1964 and, although not as forceful a personality as Tierney, he exercised the same control over the college and concurred fully with his policies for its development. In the subsequent merger debates he showed himself to be an adroit strategist and negotiator.

The initial report of the Commission had recommended that UCD, along with the other colleges of the NUI, should become an independent university. Thus one of the great aims of UCD was to be realised and the college was to be freed from the shackles of the 1908 Universities Act. However, the report had been relatively timid in its approach to Trinity College and, apart from recommending that its governing structures should resemble those of the other Irish universities, it had not made any substantial proposals for significant changes there. In particular, it had rejected suggestions that there should be any kind of merger between the two Dublin university colleges.

The idea of such a merger had not been specifically advocated by UCD in Michael Tierney's submission to the Commission. However, it is reasonable to believe that proposals for a merger which had been expressed by a number of commentators in the past would have found favour with Dr Tierney and his close colleagues in UCD.[14] An example of such views was contained in General Costello's reservation to the Commission report. In the summary of his reservation he had

13 McCartney, op. cit., Chapter 9, provides an extended treatment of the UCD merger debate.
14 Commission on Higher Education Report Vols. 1 and 2, 1967, pp. 891-900.

written:

> Our limited resources make it impossible for [Ireland] to support more than three universities at the level of staffing, accommodation and equipment required to attain and maintain high standards.
> For this reason and to end the wasteful and otherwise undesirable competition between TCD and UCD I recommend the establishment of a new University of Dublin absorbing both of them

In the complete statement of his reservation, available when the full report was published later in 1967, it is clear that his proposed new university was to be a unitary one, located primarily in Belfield and with no concessions made to the maintenance of the culture of an institution which he described with much the same venom as had Michael Tierney in his submission.

It is not altogether surprising, therefore, that the President of UCD had come to the governing body meeting on 18 April with a draft statement on the Commission's findings, which reflected such views. His draft declared:

> Considerable changes in the existing structures of UCD and of TCD are recommended by the Commission on Higher Education. The making of these changes would cause much disturbance in the working of the institutions concerned without, we believe, any promise of the advantages which might accrue from a more thorough and radical procedure. Though aware that the existence of two teaching universities in Dublin is the cause of much costly duplication, the Commission proposes no effective remedy for this. It is plain, however, that if the duplication continues, it must become increasingly harmful to both institutions and to the country. Public criticism of the recommendations has already settled on this point.
>
> Further, it does not appear that the recommendations would make available to UCD, in its proposed university status, a proper and natural title corresponding to those which will be assumed at once by the new universities in Cork and Galway.
>
> We believe that the time has come when the Dublin university question, now more than a century old, should be finally settled by the foundation of a new University of Dublin, in which the separate identities of the two existing institutions would completely disappear, and which would pool all their resources, intellectual, material and financial, under a single authority. We believe that this can be done with good will on all sides and without injustice to anyone, and that it would be productive of very great benefits to higher education and to all the interests of the country.

University College Dublin, as at present constituted, being by far the largest university institution in the Republic of Ireland, is prepared to do everything possible towards this end.[15]

The President proposed to the Governing Body that this statement, drafted as a response to the Commission's report, should be issued immediately, with the necessary contextual alterations, as a response to the Minister's merger proposal.

In the debate on the proposal, no member of the Governing Body is recorded as having expressed outright opposition to its central thrust, namely that UCD and TCD should be brought together as a single unified university. There were, however, some members who were cautious and who felt that an immediate rejection of the Minister's proposal might not be politically wise. Despite these arguments it was eventually agreed that the draft statement, appropriately re-written to take account of the changed circumstances, should be issued that day.

The final statement, as re-drafted, opened by expressing agreement with the Minister's view that 'the existence of two teaching universities in Dublin is the cause of much wasteful duplication' but continued by expressing the view that the benefits sought by the Minister would be best achieved by the complete unification of UCD and TCD. The statement continued as in the President's draft but with a nod to possible Trinity sensitivities by removing the threat that 'the separate identities of the two existing institutions would completely disappear' and the reference to UCD 'as at present constituted, being by far the largest university institution in the Republic of Ireland'.[16] The proposal by the President to issue the statement immediately was finally accepted by the governing body with only three dissenting votes.[17]

The final outcome of this meeting might be characterised as a victory for the President in getting the Governing Body to agree so enthusiastically to a hardline stance which made minimal concessions to the sensitivities of the members of Trinity College. However, some members of the Governing Body were not happy with this approach and, as the debate developed outside Board and Governing Body,

15 UCD Governing Body Minutes, 18 April 1967, UCD archives, GU2/27.
16 UCD Governing Body Minutes, 9 May 1967, UCD archives, GU2/27
17 Ibid.

adopted a position which was quite contrary to the President's 'unitary' attitude to the merger. This alternative view became particularly crystallised in the debates of the ASA and of IFUT.

At the next meeting of the Governing Body on 9 May, the President got agreement on the membership of a group which would represent the college in any negotiations which might take place on the merger. The members were to be, in addition to himself, the registrar, Dr Tom Murphy, the secretary and bursar, Joe McHale, the dean of the Science Faculty, Professor Tom Nevin, and the dean of the Commerce Faculty, Professor James Meenan. The President reported that, in the interim, he had met several people from Trinity, including the Provost, but that he had not thought it to be 'useful or prudent to have any discussion with them on the main issues'. When asked for his views on the desirability of staff from UCD having discussions with their colleagues in Trinity, he gave as his opinion that 'We should be very friendly and ready for discussion, but should avoid any definite proposals until the position was much clearer.'[18]

Alternative UCD views were beginning to emerge when the ASA held a seminar on the issue of the merger on 13 May. These views ranged from those of Eoin O'Malley,[19] a member of the Commission on Higher Education, who defended the recommendations of the Commission that four independent universities should be established, to those of Professor Maurice Kennedy[20] who believed that the whole merger idea was subversive of university autonomy. Very little support for the Governing Body plan was expressed.[21]

On 29 May, the Minister made a speech at the annual dinner of IFUT, held in the Dining Hall in Trinity, in which he sought support from the academic staff of the universities for his vision of the future. Having spelled out the financial framework within which the merger proposal had been made he asked the members of IFUT 'in the name of truth, of scholarship, of the advancement of knowledge, and of their profession as university teachers to take a hand constructively in the

---

18 Ibid.
19 Eoin O'Malley was Professor of Surgery at UCD.
20 Maurice Kennedy was a Professor of Mathematics; he succeeded Tom Murphy as Registrar when the latter was appointed President.
21 McCartney, op. cit.

shaping of the future university of Dublin and to smooth the path of the negotiations.'[22]

The next meeting of the Governing Body on 1 June preceded a formal meeting of the body with the Minister at which he spelled out in some detail his thoughts on the merger as they had developed since 18 April. This meeting was a counterpart to the later meeting on 7 June of the Minister with the Board in Trinity which has been described above. As at the Trinity meeting, the Minister presented a paper outlining his developing thoughts on the merger process. His emphasis on the need for a strong university with two, relatively, weak colleges was, presumably, not completely abhorrent to the members of the Governing Body who had favoured the idea of complete unification. Similarly, his wish that there be single faculties, which were faculties of the university, and which were divided between the colleges on the basis of the accommodation available in each site suggested, perhaps, that unification might be a goal achievable by the back door.

The Minister's proposals were debated at the next meeting of the Governing Body on 22 June. In opening the discussion, the President was adamant that in the merged university there must be only one department in each subject area. He stated that 'any departure from this complementary system, the duplication of any Faculty, for example to have Arts in Belfield and also in College Green, would not only mean that unification failed in that area, but would make it more difficult in other faculties.'[23] Discussion of the issues revealed the emergence of a dissident group on the Governing Body whose thinking diverged significantly from the views of the President and who rejected his plans for the *de facto*, if not *de jure*, unification of the Dublin colleges. In his autobiography Garret FitzGerald described how a group of nine members of the Governing Body would meet in his house before meetings to discuss strategies.[24]

A specific proposal was made by Dr Patrick Lynch[25] that there

22 O'Connor, op. cit., p.180.
23 UCD Governing Body Minutes, 22 June 1967, UCD archives, GU2/27.
24 Garret FitzGerald (1991) *All in a Life* Dublin, Gill & Macmillan, p. 57.
25 Patrick Lynch was a Professor of Economics. He had been director of both the Investment in Education and the Science and Irish Economic Development investigations for government.

should be Faculties of Arts and Science in each of the colleges and this view was supported by Garret FitzGerald and Professor John O'Donnell.[26] The proposal was opposed by the President, the Secretary and the Registrar who claimed that this plan would hark back to the Commission's ideas, which, they pointed out, had been rejected by the Minister.[27]

At a resumption of this meeting on 29 June, the President reported that he had been invited to address a meeting of the ASA two days earlier, the agenda for which contained a copy of a resolution which was to be considered at the meeting. The resolution, which had been proposed by two members of the Governing Body, Professors John O'Donnell and Desmond Williams,[28] asked the association to support the view that 'each college must retain a wide range of faculties and subjects, including the principal Arts and Science subjects.' The President had initially refused to speak to the meeting because of the appearance of this resolution although, when the proposers withdrew it, he did address the meeting and went on to express his view that 'a motion such as this one should not be proposed by members of the Governing Body while the Governing Body was discussing this very matter and had not yet made up its mind on it.'[29] At that meeting of the ASA on 27 June, a subcommittee of the association was established to consider the merger proposals and to prepare a document setting out its views on the best way forward.[30]

At the conclusion of the 29 June meeting of the Governing Body, the President said that he would now meet with faculties and with members of the junior staff[31] to explain the Governing Body position. It was his hope that when the matter had been thought about, the views of the Governing Body would be better understood and that there would not, ultimately, be any difference of opinion. As these

---

26 John O'Donnell was Professor of Chemical Engineering. He had been a member of the Steering Committee on Technical Education.

27 UCD Governing Body Minutes, 22 June 1967, UCD archives, GU2/27.

28 Desmond Williams was Professor of Modern History. He was the first Chairman of the ASA at UCD and was subsequently Chairman of IFUT.

29 UCD Governing Body Minutes, 29 June 1967, UCD archives, GU2/27.

30 McCartney, op. cit., p. 328.

31 In UCD at that time, the use of the terms senior and junior referring to staff, corresponded to the use of the terms statutory and non-statutory as described earlier.

meetings could not take place over the summer, the initiation of negotiation meetings with representatives from Trinity College could not take place until later in the year.

It was not until 31 October that the Governing Body met again to consider developments on the merger issue. By then, the President had met with all the ten faculties, and with the academic council. At each of these bodies, of which the President was, *ex officio*, Chairman, a motion had been tabled which supported the stance taken by the President and the Governing Body. It was reported that only in the Faculties of Arts and of Law had there been any significant dissension. In the Faculty of Arts, the largest in the college, only eight members opposed the motion but in the Faculty of Law, the smallest in terms of staff numbers, the motion had been defeated. It had been accepted unanimously in the other faculties and in the academic council. The President was therefore in a position to say that 'The Senior staff of the College was prepared to contemplate a system of merged departments and faculties and it seemed that few members of staff had any objection to the Minister's idea of two complementary colleges.'[32] For Dr Hogan, the concept of 'two complementary colleges' meant, essentially, that there would be no duplication of departments or faculties.

A motion was put to the meeting which proposed that:

> The Governing Body has considered the statement of the Minister for Education on the 18th of April and his paper to the Governing Body on the 1st of June and the Report of the Faculties and of the Academic Council, concerning the merger ... and is prepared to explore the principle of unified departments and faculties in one college or the other. The Governing Body further resolves to investigate other possible solution of the University question.

This was carried by 15 votes to 9. A second motion, proposed by two members of the dissident group stated:

> That the Governing Body is prepared to explore a merger based on single departments and faculties. That it does not however express any view as to whether this is or is not the best solution to the establishment of a single university with two colleges and if this solution is not acceptable, it will consider other possible solutions to the establishment of a single university with two colleges.

---

32 UCD Governing Body Minutes, 31 October 1967, UCD archives, GU2/28.

This motion was defeated by the same margin. The supporters of this alternative resolution, the so-called 'FitzGerald conspirators', much to the annoyance of the President and his supporters, decided to send a 'minority report' to the Minister outlining a more nuanced response to the merger proposal. Their report set out their reasoning and their preference for having two substantial colleges 'each of which would have a core of key arts subjects together with physics and chemistry.'[33]

In November and December the UCD ASA met to consider the document prepared by the subcommittee it had established on 27 June; the document, as amended, was finally presented to the Governing Body and the Minister on 22 January.[34] The document, while not coming down in favour of the Minister's proposals, argued strongly that, if the merger was to go ahead, there should be strong Arts and Science faculties in both colleges but that the professional schools should be merged and located in one or other college. The document had been endorsed unanimously at large meetings of the association.[35]

Negotiations between the two colleges

By late autumn the stage was set for direct negotiations between the two colleges. The thinking of the various participants in the debate had been outlined in a special issue of the journal *Studies* which was published in the summer of 1967.[36]

The 'establishment' UCD position was stated forcefully in a contribution from the Secretary and Bursar, J. P. McHale. In explaining the Governing Body's instantaneous acceptance of the idea of a complete merger of the two colleges he said that[37]:

> If the decision of Trinity College, just prior to 1908, not to take part in a university complex for Dublin has been termed the Great Refusal, the current decision on the part of University College could as aptly be termed the Great Acceptance. That a university institution should agree to liquidate itself as a separate entity in order that a new and better university structure should rise, phoenix-like, from the ashes, is a very unusual occurrence.

33 FitzGerald (1991) op. cit.
34 McCartney, op. cit., p. 328.
35 Ibid.
36 *Studies*, Summer 1967.
37 Ibid. pp. 122–3.

He went on to describe the functioning of the federal system of which UCD was a part—the National University—and explained why he did not believe that a new federal system, however structured, could achieve the rationalisation the Minister aimed for, unless it was dominated by outside, non-university, interests. He then outlined how he thought a new, completely unified, institution could function.

The Trinity viewpoint was represented by Professor Basil Chubb, although, as he noted, there was not, as yet, an official Trinity stance on the question. He said that the Minister's emphasis on preserving the identities of both colleges had led to an, initially, favourable response to his proposal but pointed to growing doubts in his college, particularly in the light of the 'official' response from UCD. He continued by stating 'To be frank … a unitary university would not be accepted by Trinity' and continued by quoting favourably from a correspondent in the *Sunday Independent* who had written that if the recommendations of UCD were to be accepted, they would result sooner or later in the effective and gradual elimination of what Trinity represented in culture, traditions and staff. He described the UCD stance as a wish to impose a 'takeover' of Trinity and he raised the spectre of the potential loss to Irish life of Trinity's contribution which he described as 'to add variety to Irish culture and to help combat the dreary and stifling conformity that is, perhaps, the greatest danger to this nation.'[38]

The *Studies* issue included articles by a number of significant commentators, including members of the Commission on Higher Education and members of staff of both colleges. A contribution by Denis Donoghue, professor of English at UCD, illustrated that, whereas there was a consensus among the officers and official bodies within UCD in favour of the 'complete unification plan', this did not mean that there was unanimity among the staff of the college. He explained:

> … it should be noted at once that the Governing Body does not accurately represent the teaching staff of University College, Dublin. At a rough count, less than half the members are currently university teachers. The teachers in UCD are represented, officially, by the Academic Council and the several faculties; unofficially by the Academic Staff Association. … at a meeting of the Academic Staff Association on 12 May 1967, it emerged

---

38 Ibid., p. 130.

without a shadow of a doubt that the majority of the teachers in UCD do not consider themselves accurately represented by the Governing Body statement of 18 April. They favour one University, two Colleges. So do I.[39]

The Minister had established a mechanism whereby, when the two colleges had sent to him memoranda on their initial thoughts on the merger, meetings would take place under the chairmanship of Dr Tarlach Ó Raifeartaigh, the Secretary of the Department of Education. As discussed above, Trinity had submitted a detailed memorandum to the Minister on 1 August. UCD was going through the process of consultation with the various internal bodies and did not make its submission until November. When it did so, to the obvious annoyance of Trinity, it consisted only of the Governing Body resolution of 31 October and a brief statement made by Dr Hogan, at a conferring ceremony in UCD, which said, *inter alia*, that 'we in University College are very far from thinking of the future university of Dublin as a mere extension or aggrandisement of our institution; we see it as something different and greater, whose success depends on Trinity's whole-hearted participation and on ours.'[40]

The first meeting of the negotiating teams did not take place until 10 November, some seven months after the Minister's initial pronouncement.[41] In Trinity, the Board was kept fully informed of the progress of negotiation but, it would appear, there was little progress to report other than an exchange of views. By contrast, no report on the meetings was minuted as having been given to the Governing Body in UCD. At least five meetings took place between 10 November and 17 February at the end of which the sides agreed to circulate within the colleges the documents which had, by then, been prepared by the two teams. These documents were referred to in subsequent discussion as 'the Trinity plan' and 'the UCD plan'.

The UCD plan was based on the Minister's tentative proposal of 1 June whereby Arts and Science would go to UCD but, in addition,

39 Ibid., p. 161.
40 TCD Board Registers Companion Volume, p. 110/111, TCD archives, MUN/V/6/13.
41 From Trinity, the representatives were the Provost and the Senior Lecturer together with Professor William Watts, Dr Brian McMurray and Professor Louden Ryan. The UCD team was made up of the President, Registrar and Secretary with Professor James Meenan and Professor Thomas Nevin.

UCD would get Engineering, Architecture and Agriculture. Trinity, under this plan, would be left with Medicine, Veterinary Medicine, Dentistry, Law, Social Science and Commerce. The Trinity proposals were, understandably, more complex. Under the Trinity plan, English, History and French would remain in both colleges with the remaining Arts subjects to be allocated between the colleges. In the Social Sciences and Commerce, Trinity would retain Economics, Politics, Psychology and Sociology while UCD would have Economics, Business Studies and Administration. Maths would be retained in both colleges. There would be a functional division in the science and applied science areas with biological and medical sciences, including Dentistry, going to Trinity while UCD would have the experimental sciences—Physics, Chemistry and Geology—in addition to Engineering, Architecture, Agriculture and Veterinary Medicine.

When these two plans were referred to the Governing Body in UCD at its meeting on 29 February 1968, it was decided to refer them to each of the faculties and to the academic council and to a meeting of the non-statutory college lecturers and assistant lecturers, to determine their views on the issues.[42] Meetings of these bodies took place over the next month. Given the complexity of the issues being debated, it is not surprising that the picture which emerged from this process of consultation with the staff of the college was somewhat confused. At the Academic Council, for example, 31 members favoured one or other of the plans while 25 members thought that neither plan was acceptable and four members abstained. However, when asked to choose between the two plans, 37 members favoured the UCD plan while nobody voted for the Trinity plan. At the Arts Faculty meeting, neither plan was deemed to be acceptable. At the meeting of the non-statutory staff, 56 members voted against both plans while only 23 members voted in favour of one or other of the plans. When asked to vote between the two plans, 49 voted in favour of the UCD plan while 13 favoured the Trinity plan.[43]

Despite the confusion of the voting procedures, when the matter came back to the Governing Body at the end of the process on 19 March, the President was able to claim that a majority of the staff

---

42 Governing Body Minutes, 29 February 1968, UCD archives, GU2/28.
43 Governing Body Minutes, 19 March 1968, UCD archives, GU2/28.

favoured the UCD scheme over the Trinity scheme. When he asked the Governing Body for its views on the two plans, 16 members voted in favour of the UCD proposals while nobody voted for the Trinity plan. Nine members—presumably the 'FitzGerald conspirators' referred to above—asked to be recorded as regarding neither plan as acceptable. The President was then given a mandate to continue the negotiation with Trinity and the government.[44]

In Trinity, copies of the plans were distributed to all staff of the college on 22 February and were discussed at length at two successive meetings of the Board.[45] In his presentation to the Board, the Provost explained the process which had led to this point. He noted that the Trinity negotiators had endeavoured to ensure that no breakdown of the talks could be laid at Trinity's door but insisted that the UCD scheme could not ensure the preservation of Trinity's identity. He stressed the importance of Board members endeavouring to ensure that the resolutions of various staff bodies which would be studying the proposals should not be antagonistic to the Minister. No purpose would be served, he said, by unconstructive rejection of all proposals.

In general discussion at the Board on 21 and 24 February, various members stated that the UCD proposals were unacceptable. Professor Moody stated that the preservation of the identity of Trinity would not be adequately covered by either scheme. He considered that the negotiators should not have been intimidated by the Minister. Professor Otway-Ruthven reported that the executive committee of the non-Fellow professors had been unanimous in rejecting both schemes. Professor Dawson[46] reported that the ASA had been gravely concerned about the proposals in the TCD scheme and had been unanimous in rejecting the Trinity memorandum [of explanation of the TCD plans] as a 'pathetic production'. His committee considered that there should have been an effort to maintain equal resources on both campuses and declared that the 'support of the Irish Federation of University Teachers and of the UCD Staff Association would have justified such a stand.' The Registrar poured some cold water on the

---

44 Ibid.
45 TCD Board Registers, 21 and 24 February 1968, TCD archives, MUN/V/5/35.
46 Professor George Dawson was the Chairman of the Trinity ASA at that time and the following year was elected as Chairman of IFUT.

most extreme proposals of opposition by noting:

> Studies under way before the Minister's announcement had indicated that our resources would not permit continuing in the manner which had been customary in recent years.... Whether by way of the effects of the merger, or through the effects of not securing continued support at our present level from Government sources, hard decisions would have to be taken.[47]

No vote is recorded in the minutes of the meeting but it can be assumed that the feeling of the meeting was overwhelmingly in favour of the negotiators continuing to fight strongly against the UCD proposals.

At the next meeting of the Board on 6 March 1968, it was reported that, in response to the circulation to staff of the two college plans, resolutions had been received from the Students' Representative Council, the scholars in committee, the non-Fellow professors, the School of Natural Sciences, the Readers and Lecturers' Association, the ASA, the junior Fellows and the Faculty of Arts. It was then resolved:

> That before negotiations of the future University of Dublin are resumed, machinery will be evolved for consultations with the Deans and Heads of Department upon the progress of negotiations and the development of College policy therein. In the interim, a committee consisting of the College representatives, the Deans and the Chairman of the [Academic] Staff Association or his deputy will consider any developments.[48]

It is interesting to note the difference in the approach of the two colleges to the ASA and to IFUT which represented the great majority of the academic staff in both colleges. At the meeting of the UCD Governing Body on 30 January, 1968 the Secretary reported that he had received a letter from the Chairman of the ASA together with copies of a memorandum on the merger, for distribution to the members of the Governing Body. The Secretary said that he could not circulate them because 'the ASA was not an official body of our College. Copies were available for anyone who wanted one.'[49] By contrast, in Trinity, the chair of the ASA was inducted as a *de facto* member of the negotiating team. This difference of approach illustrates a difference

47 TCD Board Registers, 21 and 24 February 1968, TCD archives, MUN/V/5/35.
48 Ibid. 75/1.
49 UCD Governing Body Minutes, 30 January 1968, UCD archives, GU/2/28.

in the way authority was exercised in the two colleges. It also points to the fact that, increasingly, the opposition shown by the staff association in UCD and by IFUT to the UCD Governing Body's approach to the merger would be crucial to Trinity's efforts to win the political battles that lay ahead with the Minister and with the wider public.

All the plans of both sides were thrown into disarray by the sudden death of the Minister, Donogh O'Malley, aged only 47, on 10 March 1968. O'Malley had been a dynamic reforming minister, firstly, in the Department of Health and then in Education. Sean O'Connor, who had worked closely with O'Malley as Assistant Secretary in the Department of Education, described him as the folk-hero of Irish education. 'His gestures were always on the grand scale and timed to obtain maximum publicity. Almost always they were on the side of "the common man" and against authoritarian structures that bore down on him. And O'Malley was all the more a hero because he had common failings.'[50] While it is true that, unlike his plans for the introduction of free secondary education, his merger proposals on 18 April had been brought to and approved by cabinet prior to their announcement, it is unlikely that another minister in that government would have had the energy and enthusiasm to get them so far so quickly. It was now up to his successor, Brian Lenihan, to try and bring his plans to fruition.

50 O'Connor op. cit.

(L–r) Brian Lenihan, Charles Haughey and Michael O'Kennedy at a press conference in the late 1960s (The Irish Times)

6. The Lenihan plan

Brian Lenihan was, with Donogh O'Malley, part of a new generation of Fianna Fáil politicians who gradually replaced the founding fathers of that political party through the 1960s. He had served for four years as Minister for Justice when he was thrust into the Education portfolio on the death of O'Malley in March 1968. His first major task as Minister for Education was to bring to fruition his predecessor's plans for the merger of UCD and TCD.

In both colleges, the next few months were a period of marking time while the new minister familiarised himself with his brief. In Trinity, the Board had established a merger committee to oversee future developments and negotiations. The Board also agreed that, if IFUT were to apply to the Minister for a place at the negotiating table, Trinity would support such an application. In UCD, the Governing Body absorbed the outcome of the consultation process which had been undertaken within the college. In July, Mr Lenihan announced details of his development of the merger proposals in what came to be called 'the Lenihan plan' or 'the 6 July plan'.[1]

Initially, the Lenihan plan declared its support for three key elements of the Report of the Commission on Higher Education. These were:

1) that the NUI should be dissolved and that UCC and UCG should be constituted as separate universities;

2) that a permanent authority be established to deal with the financial and organisational problems of higher education;

3) that there be established a Conference of Irish Universities to deal principally, with academic problems common to all the university institutions.

The plan then proceeded to elaborate on the skeletal proposals contained in the O'Malley merger statement. In doing so, it claimed to be based particularly on the existing student numbers in each area

---

[1] The plan was actually published on 5 July, but the discussion began the following day.

in each of the colleges. Its key points with regard to the allocation of faculties and departments were as follows:

1) *Arts* The present range of subjects in each college would continue to be taught there, subject to the condition that, as circumstances permitted, the complete fusion of the teaching and study of small subjects[2] would be effected.

2) *Science* Each college was to retain its existing range of disciplines, but the main centre for experimental sciences[3] would be in UCD and the main centre for the biological sciences would be in Trinity.

3) *Medicine, veterinary medicine, dentistry, pharmacy and physiotherapy* These were to be located entirely in Trinity College.

4) *Engineering, commerce and social science* These were to go entirely to UCD.

5) *Law* This was to go to Trinity.

6 *Agriculture and architecture* These were to go entirely to UCD.

7) *Mathematics and statistics* These were to be in both colleges although postgraduate work should be primarily located in one or other college.

8) *Theology and divinity* Just as was the case with the Commission on Higher Education, definitive statements on these areas were not advanced; however, St Patrick's College, Maynooth was seen as having a place in the eventual solution for this area of study.

While the detailed elaboration of the Lenihan plan lacked the rhetorical flourishes of the O'Malley announcement, it did conclude with the stirring sentence: 'Finally, the tale will go far beyond our shores of how Irishmen of diverse traditions have found the way to harmonious collaboration in the moral and intellectual development, at the highest level, of the nation's youth.'

Reaction to the Lenihan plan

The publication of the Lenihan plan changed radically the terms of the merger debate. In the case of Trinity College, it was now to retain all its studies in the Arts area and their association with the copyright

---

2 The statement did not attempt a definition of smallness.

3 The term 'experimental sciences' was a synonym for what would today be more commonly referred to as the physical sciences; it referred to Physics, Chemistry and Geology.

library[4] in the college was assured. In the sciences, it was to lose the departments of physics, chemistry and geology. However, despite an illustrious history in these areas, particularly in physics and geology, they were not at that time the most prestigious of the Trinity schools. In return, it was to have a monopoly on the biological sciences. In terms of the professional schools, Trinity was to get the high-status faculties of Law and Medicine, together with the other para-medical schools of dentistry, pharmacy, physiotherapy and veterinary medicine. It would lose engineering and commerce, in neither of which fields did it have great strength, although it would also lose social studies where its development of sociological studies would have been seen as distinct from those in UCD. Overall, this was a plan that Trinity could accept.

By contrast, the reaction to the Lenihan plan in UCD was one of dismay. The grand ambitions of the Governing Body to be the dominant force in a largely unified institution, centred in the new Belfield campus, were to be no more. Instead, UCD was to gain nothing from the merger except a monopoly of the faculties of Engineering and Commerce and was to lose the faculties of Law and Medicine. The threatened loss of the latter was a particular source of consternation, given the dominant role of the medical school in the history and the development of the college and its still central role in Irish society.

In its concern over the implications of the Lenihan plan, the Governing Body was no longer to be seen as isolated from the general body of academic staff in UCD represented by the ASA. Whereas the ASA members might previously have been partly motivated by a distrust of the Governing Body establishment and by a liberal inclination to protect their separated brethren in Trinity, the new plan threatened the appalling vista of a UCD which was less complete in terms of academic diversity and poorer in social esteem, in competition with a rejuvenated Trinity College. Just as Donogh O'Malley had, for the first time, brought about a kind of unity of purpose between the academic staffs of the two colleges, Brian Lenihan had unwittingly brought about a similar accord between the staff and the

---

4 The Library of Trinity College, after the establishment of the Irish state in 1922, had retained the right, along with a number of British libraries, to be given copies of every publication produced in the United Kingdom and Ireland.

governors of UCD. McCartney records details of a correspondence between President Hogan of UCD and the Minister in which Dr Hogan labelled the plan as a pure and simple *diktat* and claimed that the new plan was essentially what had been sought by the Board of Trinity College.

On the day the Minister announced his proposals IFUT was holding a seminar in Maynooth to consider the relative merits of various proposals for the future of higher education in Ireland, While unable to examine the plan in any detail due to the lack of prior notice, a statement was issued following the seminar which stated, in part, that 'the Seminar, by a large majority approved, as being in the best interests of higher education in Ireland, the recommendation of the Commission on Higher Education in favour of the establishment of UCD, TCD, UCC and UCG as independent universities.' The statement went on:

> The Federation had no opportunity to study in any depth the Minister's statement published today ... It noted, however, the Minister's proposals to dissolve the NUI and establish UCC and UCG as separate universities, to set up a permanent authority to deal with financial and organisational problems, and to establish a conference of Irish Universities. It approved of these proposals which accord with the recommendations of the Commission on Higher Education. The Federation also recognised that within the limits imposed by the Government's decision to associate the two Dublin Colleges in a new University of Dublin the Minister had taken into account the submissions made to him by [IFUT] and by the Staff Associations of the Colleges concerned, on the distribution of faculties and departments.[5]

Two weeks later the ASA in UCD issued a statement in which it reiterated its view that the interests of higher education in Ireland 'will best be served by four independent and closely co-operating universities.'[6] Meanwhile, the Minister was altering the mechanism of the merger debate by acting promptly on his proposal to create, 'a permanent authority ... to deal with the financial and organisational problems of higher education.' In August 1968, he announced the

---

5 Record of the Proceedings of the Seminar held in St Patrick's College Maynooth on Saturday 6 July 1968. IFUT records Filed with Minutes of the Council of IFUT for 1968–9.

6 McCartney, op. cit.

establishment of the Higher Education Authority.

The Higher Education Authority

The Report of the Commission on Higher Education had examined the mechanisms by which the institutions of higher education and research had related to the state and had been highly critical of the lack of any co-ordinated system for planning and development of the sector. A number of submissions from the universities had expressed unhappiness with a system whereby each of them presented their individual budgetary requests to the Department of Education and had these requests considered by civil servants whose main experience lay in the fields of primary and secondary education. For a model which might replace the existing system, most academic opinion in Ireland at that time looked to the University Grants Commission in Britain.

The University Grants Committee (UGC) had been established in Britain in the immediate aftermath of the First World War, with a specific mandate to act as a buffer between the universities and government in the allocation of finance. The UGC was a body whose part-time membership was largely drawn from active university staff with a full-time chairman, usually coming from an academic background, and a full-time staff largely consisting of civil servants with Treasury experience.[7] The UGC made submissions directly to the Treasury detailing the overall need for finance for the universities for the following five years and distributed the money received to the individual universities in the form of block grants.

In parallel with the development of the UGC, a Committee of Vice-Chancellors and Principals (CVCP) had developed to provide an inter-institutional relationship and to articulate a collective academic view, both to the UGC and elsewhere. Each university vice-chancellor was automatically a member of the CVCP as were the principals of

---

7 University Grants Committee (1968) *University Development 1962–67*. London: HMSO pp. 3–4. In 1968, the Chairman of the UCG, Sir John Wolfenden, was a former Vice-Chancellor of Reading University, 13 of the members were university academics, two members were from other areas of education and three came from industry

the Scottish universities. The CVCP had a small secretariat which it shared with the Association of Commonwealth Universities.⁸ As it happened, both the UGC and the CVCP were in transition, arising from the recommendations of the Robbins Report in 1963.⁹

The Report of the Commission on Higher Education had listed a large number of submissions from the university world—both from administrators and academic staff—which advocated the development of a body such as the UGC, to manage the relationship between the university and the state in Ireland. There is no evidence in the Report of any submission proposing an Irish analogue of the CVCP.

While accepting the need for a buffer between the institutions and the state, the Commission had rejected the UGC model as inappropriate for Ireland. In its analysis of future needs it saw the need for a more elaborate structure than that provided by the Grants Committee, which would have a broad planning and development function in addition to its role in distributing the financial resources which came from the state. The body, which was to have a role mirroring that of the Commission itself, was also to be called the Commission for Higher Education; it would be established by an Act of the Oireachtas and would report directly to the Taoiseach rather than to the Minister for Education. It would have a part-time chairman and eight other part-time members, none of whom would be drawn from any of the institutions which came within its scope. In addition to examining institutional budgets and plans for development and advising the government thereon it would be asked to 'keep the development of higher education under continual review, and to report, at least every five years, on the country's needs in higher education, the developments necessary to meet these needs, and possible methods of financing them.'¹⁰

The Commission had also addressed the question of inter-institutional relationships and recommended the establishment of a Council of Irish Universities. As with the comparison between the UGC

8 Aitken, op. cit., pp. 165–71.

9 In *Universities Quarterly* (Spring) 1969, there are articles by A. H. Halsey, Sir Maurice Bowra, R. C. Griffiths and Sir Robert Aitken discussing the relationship between the universities and the state in Great Britain at that time and, in particular, the role and functions of the UGC and the CVCP.

10 Ibid., p. 477.

THE LENIHAN PLAN

and the proposed permanent Commission for Higher Education, the Council proposed by the Commission was to be a much more elaborate body than its UK counterpart, the CVCP, and was to have, for example, mandatory powers in such areas as external examining and matriculation standards. The Lenihan plan now endorsed both these recommendations although with a name change in both cases; the permanent Commission on Higher Education was to be called the Higher Education Authority (HEA) and the Council of Irish Universities was to be named the Conference of Irish Universities.

In setting up the Authority the Minister altered significantly the membership of the body as recommended by the Commission. Its recommendation had been that no member of the Authority should be a staff member in any of the institutions depending on it; the Minister, in appointing its 14 part-time members picked seven members who were on the academic staff of the universities, including two each from TCD and UCD. In place of its recommended part-time chairman, the Minister appointed as full-time Chairman, Dr Tarlach Ó Raifeartaigh[11], the out-going Secretary of the Department of Education. At the opening meeting of the Authority on 12 September 1968, Mr Lenihan explained his rejection of the Commission's recommendation that members should not be associated with the universities by stating that he was sure 'that no person among you is going to be guided other than by objective appraisals.'[12]

The terms of reference for the Authority were to be modelled on the recommendations of the Commission and were, in addition to its recurrent funding role, to 'examine the existing provisions for higher education with a view to making recommendations to the Minister for Education on the necessity for the existing provisions and on the elimination of unnecessary duplication.'[13] It was significant that the HEA was to report to the Minister for Education rather than to the Taoiseach, as had been recommended by the Commission.

In his opening address to the HEA on 12 September, the Minister directed the members: 'It is now your interim task to advise me on

---

11 Tarlach Ó Raifeartaigh (1905–84).

12 Minutes of the Higher Education Authority, 12 September 1968, HEA archives, Box 1.

13 TCD Board Register Companion Volume TCD archives, MUN/V/6/13 p. 89.

the nature and form of the legislation which will be required to put into effect the decisions already taken by the Government on higher education.'[14] This immediately set off alarm bells in the universities where it was feared that the Authority was to be a blunt instrument used to implement the government plans and override the universities' objections. The academics from the Dublin colleges who had accepted places on the Authority were immediately put under pressure by their colleagues, and accused of having 'sold out' to the government. In Trinity, the Registrar, Ian Howie, had to assure the Board 'that he had given no undertaking of any kind to the Minister or to his representative in accepting the invitation to join the Authority.'[15] When challenged over the scarcity of academics from the humanities on the Authority, he assured the Board that the Conference of Irish Universities should, when set up, ensure representation over the full range of faculty interests.[16]

At the first meeting of the Authority, a letter signed by Professors Jack Grainger and Ian Howie from Trinity and Professors Patrick Lynch and Thomas Murphy from UCD was read out which stated:

> As academic members of the *ad hoc* Higher Education Authority from the two Dublin Colleges, we feel it is essential that the Minister and our fellow members of the Authority should know unequivocally from the outset the terms and conditions on which we accepted the Minister's invitation to join the Authority.... our position has been misrepresented, in particular in deductions drawn from official statements made after we had accepted the Minister's invitation...We wish to state...that we were neither asked for, nor did we give any specific undertaking to support any particular policy, in regard to Higher Education, nor, in our view does our acceptance of membership of the Authority bind us to do so.[17]

The intensity of the debate taking place was illustrated by a television programme broadcast on 11 September on RTÉ in which, as reported in *The Irish Times* the following day, a group of senior academics confronted the Minister for Education about the establish-

---

14 Minutes of the Higher Education Authority, 12 September 1968, HEA archives, Box 1.
15 TCD Board Register 28 August 1968, TCD archives, MUN/V/5/35.
16 Ibid.
17 Minutes of the Higher Education Authority, 12 September 1968, HEA archives, Box 1.

ment of the HEA. Denis Donoghue is reported as having claimed that the authority had been constituted 'on the basic condition that the Lenihan Plan was acceptable to all members of the Authority—and not just to a majority of them.'[18] Despite the eminence of his opponents, the consensus view afterwards was that the Minister had been a clear winner of the debate.

The debate was taken a stage further a week later when a letter signed by 467 academic staff members of the Irish universities was published in the *Irish Independent* and *The Irish Times*, which both also ran editorials on the subject.[19] The key element of the letter was a rejection of the Lenihan plan and a statement of the belief of the signatories that the development of higher education in Ireland could best be served by a system of four or more separate and co-operating universities. It went on to claim that 'to impose an artificial unity on these two [Dublin] colleges by forcing them into a single administrative structure which they do not need and do not want would be both educationally and administratively unsound.' The *Irish Independent* editorial noted:

> We recently heard Mr Brian Lenihan commend his Higher Education Authority to public approval because of the distinguished people from the academic world who had agreed to serve upon it. We look now to the Minister to apply the same measure when he takes up the statement published this morning and signed by forty times as many university teachers as have accepted nomination to the Authority.

The *Irish Times* editorial on the issue was less supportive of the academic protesters. It read, in part:

> Several things are now obvious ... The first is that the economic argument for the merger ... has been seriously questioned, even by economists like Mr Garret FitzGerald who agree with the idea of a merger in principle. In the second place, the educational advantages of a large university involving at least two and possibly four different units in Dublin has been seriously

---

18 *The Irish Times* 12 September 1968. The story in *The Irish Times* lists the academic participants in the programme as Professors Basil Chubb and George Dawson of Trinity, Professors John O'Meara and Denis Donoghue, Dr Garret FitzGerald and Mr J. P. McHale from UCD, Professor Frank Ford from UCG, Professor Richard Breathnach from UCC, Professor F. S. L. Lyons of the University of Sussex and others.

19 21 September 1968.

questioned by people whose experience of teaching at the university level must be respected.

These two objections must, however, be examined in the context of what many people feel to have been Donogh O'Malley's basic motivation; the ending of what he described as 'this insidious form of partition on our own doorstep'.

In a sense it now seems . . . as if this last argument, the social and religious one, will be of decisive importance. . . . The weight, in our opinion, is on the side of the merger.

The battle lines were now clearly drawn. UCD strongly opposed the Lenihan plan of 6 July and had abandoned its earlier support for the O'Malley vision of a united university in Dublin. In its opposition, it had found unanimity between the Governing Body establishment and the general body of academic staff represented by the ASA.[20] The Board in Trinity were clearly pleased with the Lenihan plan and proceeded to engage with the HEA in the spirit of the plan; on the other hand, a number of the members of the academic staff in Trinity, who had been strongly opposed to O'Malley, continued their opposition to any merger and were happy to pursue the IFUT goal of 'four, or more, separate and co-operating universities'.[21] This divided opinion between the colleges was reflected at the meeting of the Council of IFUT on 16 November. Garret FitzGerald and others from UCD complained that a report had been widely circulated in UCD stating that the Trinity negotiators had conveyed the impression to the HEA that the staff association of TCD accepted the Minister's proposed faculty distribution and were, with the negotiators, insisting upon the allocation of Medicine and Law to TCD. Professor Dawson responded that the ASA in Trinity had made no such recommendation but had accepted the Lenihan distribution, only insofar as it felt that in the context of two independent and co-operating universities in Dublin each should contain not less than the degree of duplicated teaching provided for in

20 From this point on the Governing Body was happy to receive and consider letters and reports from the staff association which, prior to 6 July, they had neither acknowledged nor recognised.

21 Over the next few months, the Board received submissions from the Fellows, regretting the Board's stance on the 6 July plan, from the RLA complaining about the unrepresentative nature of the Authority and from the ASA echoing IFUT's call for four independent universities. TCD archives, *Board Register Companion Volume* MUN/V/6/13.

the plan. This clarification was accepted by the UCD delegates.[22]

At its third meeting on 29 October, the Registrar of Trinity, Ian Howie, informed the HEA that 'as far as attitudes to the government's proposals in TCD were concerned, the position was worsening from the Authority's point of view.'[23] He reminded the authority that a very large number of TCD staff had signed the newspaper letter of 21 September and said that, following the results of elections to the Board, it could not be assumed that it would maintain the attitude it had adopted consistently; it could not ignore majority opinion among the staff.[24]

In an outspoken letter to the Minister on 17 September, the President of UCD praised the approach of O'Malley, and criticised Brian Lenihan, stating, 'It seems to me that the new scheme may be a result of the principle that when something is attempted and found too difficult, the easiest way out is to do anything at all that may look like the original proposal and then hope for the best.' In concluding his lengthy letter he wrote: 'may I say that while you hold that discussion of the new scheme is at an end, I think that, if the interest of the country is considered, thought and discussion have barely begun.' In his reply, Mr Lenihan admonished the President:

> I feel it is incumbent on me in regard to the view expressed in the final paragraph of your letter that 'thought and discussion have barely begun' to stress that in the matter of the future provision for higher education in Dublin you, in the position which you occupy, are no less a servant of the people than I am. As far as I am concerned, the will of the people will be expressed in Dáil Éireann through legislation setting up one university in Dublin.[25]

At a meeting of the UCD Academic Council on 11 October, a resolution was passed which urged the Governing Body negotiators 'to keep open all possible methods of co-ordinating the activities of the two existing university institutions in Dublin, including the plan for two universities in Dublin. This resolution was endorsed at a

---

22 IFUT Minutes of Council Meeting, 16 November 1968. Professor Dawson was a member of the Trinity merger committee and, therefore, one of the Trinity negotiators.
23 HEA Minutes, 29 October 1968, HEA archives, Box 1.
24 Ibid.
25 UCD Governing Body Minutes, 15 October 1968, UCD archives, GU2/28.

meeting of the Governing Body four days later which also praised the President for his letter of 17 September.[26]

At the next meeting of the Governing Body, the President gave a report on the first meeting of the UCD negotiation team with the HEA on 13 November. He observed that 'during the meeting it began to appear that the Authority was not sure whether it could listen to arguments on the merits of the proposed scheme or whether it was confined to considering the best method of implementing the scheme.'[27] He had subsequently written to the HEA Chairman to seek assurances that 'if the College representatives went back again, they could discuss the merits of the scheme'.[28]

At the same meeting, Professor James Meenan argued that when the universities talked about four independent and co-operating universities, they should begin to state positively how this co-operation was to be brought about. In the course of an extended debate on this point Garret FitzGerald noted that the Minister had advanced two main arguments in support of his plan, namely, the saving of money and the improvements which would result in the teaching delivered to the 'boys and girls of Ireland'.[29] He proposed that, 'if the college could take the initiative and state that it was willing to achieve these aims without any kind of merger, and that it would investigate the possibilities of co-operation in the use of equipment and in the cross-registration of students, the announcement could transform the public atmosphere about the merger.'[30] It was generally agreed that the mechanisms for co-operation should be explored further.

Given the strained relationship between the two Dublin colleges and the outright hostility of the UCD Governing Body to the government proposals, the HEA was happy to accept IFUT as an independent academic voice in the on-going debate and it engaged in detailed

---

26 Ibid. At that meeting it was agreed to replace Dr Thomas Murphy as one of its negotiators, in view of the fact that he had been appointed as a member of the HEA, by the Dean of the Medical Faculty, Dr D. K. O'Donovan.

27 UCD Governing Body Minutes, 19 November 1968, UCD archives, GU2/29.

28 Ibid.

29 At the time, the Minister was the subject of a certain amount of scorn in university circles for his repeated use of the phrase 'the boys and girls of Ireland' as the object of his concern in bringing forward the 6 July proposals.

30 Ibid.

THE LENIHAN PLAN

discussion with the Federation on the range of issues which arose. In response, IFUT spent most of its energies over the next six months in preparing for meetings with the HEA and in drafting documents detailing its suggestions for change. Much of this discussion centred on the role of the HEA itself and the form which legislation to establish it on a statutory basis should take.

At its meeting on 14 December, the Chairman of the Council of IFUT, Professor Desmond Williams, outlined the questions which he believed were most important at the time. These included whether the HEA should be concerned with all tertiary education or just the universities, to which government department the Authority should report and whether the Conference of Irish Universities should have mandatory powers. The Council agreed to recommend that the HEA should deal only with the universities and that it should report to the Department of Education rather than to the Taoiseach. In a debate on the Conference it was agreed that it should have a limited range of mandatory powers but only those with no financial implications.[31] At the next meeting of the Council there was a lengthy debate on whether the legislation establishing the HEA should be enacted prior to the final decision on the Dublin merger. Professor Ruaidhrí de Valera[32] argued that it was dangerous to demonstrate confidence in the HEA by agreeing to its statutory establishment before its final stance on the merger was known. However, the contrary view, articulated by Garret FitzGerald, that it was more important to influence its decisions on its own structures and powers than to try to block its establishment, was accepted by a majority.[33]

At a meeting on 23 January between an IFUT delegation and the HEA, issues connected with the establishment of the Authority and of the Conference were discussed in detail. The HEA revealed its current thinking on the Conference; it saw its mandatory powers as being limited to the control of entry standards. On the merger issue, the HEA supported the merger of professional faculties and the Lenihan distribution of these. Remarkably, it criticised IFUT for its failure to

---

31 IFUT Council Minutes, 14 December 1968. IFUT records.
32 Professor de Valera (1916–78), a son of the President of Ireland, was Professor of Archaeology in UCD.
33 IFUT Council Minutes, 6 January 1969, IFUT records.

do anything 'to persuade the Bishops to remove the ban on Trinity College.'[34] Over the next few months IFUT's major concern was the completion of a set of proposals for the internal governing structures of the universities under the new dispensation.[35]

The NUI enters the debate

On 23 November 1968, the NUI, whose abolition had been announced by Donogh O'Malley 18 months previously, finally met to consider its response to its threatened demise. The Chancellor of the NUI in 1968 was still Éamon de Valera, who had been elected months before the Treaty split in 1921; the rotating vice-chancellorship was at that time held by Dr Hogan, the President of UCD. Dr Hogan, now seeking allies in the battles being fought in Dublin, urged the Senate of the NUI to become involved. While the colleges in Cork and Galway had given a guarded welcome to the merger proposals , insofar as they had promised independence, they had not, up to now, taken any significant part in the debate. At a meeting on 23 October, the Senate agreed that it should make its views known.[36] It requested a meeting with Taoiseach Jack Lynch to discuss all matters connected with university re-organisation and, while he was initially reluctant to meet with a Senate delegation,[37] the meeting eventually took place on 6 February 1969.

At this meeting, as reported later to the UCD Governing Body by the President, Dr Hogan, who had been part of the Senate delegation, the Senate argued strongly that the NUI should not be abolished until a satisfactory solution had been found for the two Dublin colleges. Dr Hogan expressed his appreciation of the way in which the Cork and Galway members had put UCD's case very strongly. The Taoiseach had responded cautiously to requests that the terms of reference of the HEA should be changed to allow full consideration of alternatives to

---

34 IFUT Council Minutes, 1 February 1969, IFUT records.

35 IFUT Council Proposals for Revision of University Charters and Statutes. Part I Internal Government of Universities, IFUT records.

36 McCartney, op. cit., p. 333.

37 Senate of the NUI, Minutes of meeting of 9 January 1969, NUI archive. The initial response from Mr Lynch stated that 'as the HEA had been established by the Government to examine and advise it on the question of Higher Education, all matters affecting Higher Education should be addressed to the Authority alone'.

the Lenihan plan.[38] Following the meeting, the Senate sought permission from the Taoiseach to allow the same group to meet with the HEA.[39]

While UCD and its allies were engaged in a war of words with the Minister and the HEA, Trinity was proceeding positively, if cautiously, to engage with the Authority on ways to implement the Lenihan plan. On 30 October the Board endorsed, by a vote of 13 to 3, a document prepared by its merger committee which accepted the Minister's assurances that the colleges would be legal entities, each with its own identity, and which also accepted the distribution of subjects as proposed by the Minister. The Board agreed to negotiate with the HEA on this basis 'provided it was understood that its representatives had been instructed to test with the HEA all proposals under consideration by comparison with alternatives possible under a two-university solution and [that] if it became clear that the best interests of higher education would be served by that or any other solution, the Board reserved the right to press for it.'[40]

Gentle revolutions

The student revolutions of the late 1960s brought about a profound change in the way academic and political opinion throughout the world viewed the university. At that time, student organisations were not considered, either by government or by the colleges, as meriting much attention. The wave of student unrest which was then sweeping the world was to change this perception.

Significant student activism had its first public manifestation in 1964 on the Berkeley campus of the University of California. It arose from a demand for free speech on campus by groups supporting the civil rights movement and developed into a mass movement of radicalised students whose example spread to many other US universities. As the movement expanded the main focus for student concern became the US involvement in the Vietnam war so that by 1968 there were substantial outbreaks of student violence in Harvard, Columbia and

---

38 UCD Governing Body Minutes, 29 April 1969. UCD archives, GU2/29.
39 Senate of the NUI, Minutes of meeting of 24 April 1969. NUI archives. Mr Lynch was awarded an honorary degree by the NUI on 24 April.
40 TCD Board Register 30 October 1968 TCD archives, MUN/V/5/36.

other US campuses and then in Europe in London and Rome and in Eastern Europe in Warsaw and Belgrade. The most dramatic of these outbreaks occurred in Paris in May 1968 where student violence led to mass strikes and a threatened downfall of General de Gaulle's government. Dublin was not immune from these international influences.

In Trinity, a group calling itself 'The Internationalists' was set up in 1965. Initially it sought to analyse the role of the university in society and to promote academic freedom and better staff-student relations in Trinity. Along with a number of politicised students it included among its members such prominent academic staff as Kader Asmal, Owen Sheehy Skeffington and R. B. McDowell. It quickly adopted a more radical, politically hard left orientation and eventually re-named itself as the Irish Communist Movement (Marxist-Leninist) in 1969.[41] While still wearing the Internationalist label it became the focus for student activism in Trinity when it launched a protest about the visit of King Baudouin of Belgium to the campus in 1968. Despite scuffles with gárdai and sensationalist headlines in some of the Dublin papers the event did not lead to any significant radicalisation of the general body of students. Although the movement continued to exist it never had a significant effect on the college despite the oratorical efforts of its most prominent leader, David Vipond,[42] from the Dining Hall steps. Its failure to make an impact may be seen partly as a consequence of the relatively benign, collegial atmosphere of Trinity and the relatively benevolent style of its academic leadership. The Internationalists do not appear to have concerned themselves with the intricacies of the merger debate. Student activism in Trinity gradually became the preserve of the officially recognised Students' Representative Council (SRC) and in its later manifestation as the Students' Union.[43]

In UCD, rather than student activism emerging from a Marxist-Leninist analysis of society, the Student Christian Movement (SCM) was the seed from which later radical activism developed.[44] The SCM

---

41 The Internationalists were generally referred to as Maoists; an analysis of the fissiparous tendencies of radical left political groupings is outside the scope of this work.

42 David Vipond stood unsuccessfully in the 1973 Monaghan bye-election.

43 The events of the period are covered in Luce, op. cit.

44 See, for example, John Maguire in Phillip Pettit (Ed.) (1969) *The Gentle Revolution: Crisis in the universities* Dublin, Scepter Books.

promoted an analysis of the university and its place in society from a Catholic Left perspective and this provided a stimulus from which a number of students drew when they established a body called Students for Democratic Action (SDA) in 1968. Those who were involved in these moves included John Feeney,[45] Kevin Myers[46] and Ruairí Quinn.[47] The SRC, headed that year by Eddie O'Connor,[48] was involved in the events that followed although, because of its representative structures, it was frequently out-manoeuvred by the more agile SDA in promoting radical student activity.

Debate among student and staff protagonists ranged over such matters as student independence from older disciplinary structures and outmoded pedagogical frameworks. The most heated debates, however, were over the control of the university and over possible changes in its governing structures. Initially, the Student Representative Councils in Trinity and UCD had jointly welcomed the O'Malley announcement of his move towards 'rationalisation' of the university provision in Dublin.[49] The primary focus of their concern was that new structures would provide a place for students on the decision-making bodies in the university

Early signs of trouble for the college authorities in UCD arose over demands by architectural students for action to forestall the withdrawal of recognition of their degrees by the Royal Institute of British Architects[50] and by radical student protests at a conferring ceremony in October 1968 over the establishment of staff-student committees

---

45 John Feeney graduated with a BA in English. He became a journalist for various publications and edited *The Catholic Standard*. He wrote a biography of John Charles McQuaid (1974). He was killed in a plane accident in 1984.

46 Kevin Myers graduated with a BA in History. He has been a journalist with RTÉ and a columnist for *The Irish Times* and the *Irish Independent*.

47 Ruairí Quinn is an architect and Labour Party politician. First elected to Dáil Eireann in 1977 he has held various ministries including Finance and Education & Skills.

48 Eddie O'Connor is a chemical engineer who worked with the Electricity Supply Board and as Chief Executive of Bórd na Móna. He has been a key figure in the development of renewable energy resources in Ireland and internationally.

49 *Irish Press*, 19 April 1967.

50 The trouble in the School of Architecture resulted eventually in the removal from office of the head of the school (Garret FitzGerald's brother Desmond) and the dismissal of two, untenured, members of staff.

by the college.⁵¹ Not to be outdone by the SDA, the SRC decided to hold a 'teach-in' for students in the Great Hall in Earlsfort Terrace⁵² to debate the merger in November 1968. As the college authorities refused permission for this event, the SRC went ahead and occupied the space over lunch-time with, as *The Irish Times* estimated, over 2,000 students from both UCD and Trinity participating.⁵³ Staff members from both colleges also addressed the meeting.

Over the next few months competition between the SRC and the SDA continued with regular teach-ins and mass meetings and a major confrontation between college authorities and students when a meeting of the academic council was blockaded. The merger was no longer the centre of debate. The radical SDA had widened its focus to call for the abolition of the 'present elitist system of education in Ireland' so that the university could serve the interests of the people of Ireland as a whole,⁵⁴ while the SRC was, more modestly, seeking a change in the governing structures of UCD with students having membership of all significant bodies.

Matters came to a head in February and March 1969 over the alleged mismanagement of the imminent move of the Arts Faculty from Earlsfort Terrace to its new building in Belfield and the possibility that the students would be transferred prior to the provision of adequate library facilities. Dissatisfaction with the response of the authorities on this issue led to an occupation of the administrative offices of the college on 19 and 20 February 1969 and, the following week, to a general disruption of the academic activities of the college by an extended series of teach-ins and mass meetings. Garret FitzGerald, in his second autobiography—*Just Garret*—describes how the militant activism of the SDA was rapidly subverted by the more cautious reformist feelings of the majority of students.⁵⁵ The student revolution—'the Gentle Revolution', as it was named by Philip Pettit

---

51 These were seen by activist students as an attempt to forestall student unrest in the wake of the May '68 events in Paris.

52 The Great Hall is now the main auditorium of the National Concert Hall. At that time it was used primarily as a reading room for the library.

53 *The Irish Times*, 13 November 1968.

54 McCartney op. cit.

55 FitzGerald, G. (2010), *Just Garret*, Dublin, Liberties Press, pp. 114, 115.

THE LENIHAN PLAN

in a book which he edited on the events[56]—eventually petered out into a joint committee of the ASA and a student group which had been elected at a mass meeting, which met to draw up a blueprint for a future, democratic, UCD where students and academic staff would have a place in its governing structures. The ambitions of this group were partially achieved 30 years later with the provisions of the Irish Universities Act (1997). [57]

For and against the Lenihan plan

While UCD was preoccupied by student militancy, Trinity continued its collaboration with the HEA on the measures needed to implement the Lenihan plan. Apart from its guarded satisfaction with the merger proposals, Trinity's willingness to engage with the Authority was undoubtedly influenced by its need to have the good will of the HEA in securing agreement for its plans for a new Arts building. The Trinity merger committee met with the Authority in November 1968 and discussed the form of future legislation and the implications for the conditions of service for staff if and when the plan was implemented.[58] In January, the Board considered a memorandum from the Engineering School on how the merger would proceed[59] and then it considered a memorandum from the Dean of the Medical School on *Future Education in Medicine and the allied Professions in Dublin* which claimed that 'from the point of view of education in the professional faculties, important advantages will flow from the implementation of July 6th.'[60]

In June 1969 the Provost wrote to the President of UCD as follows:

> We have received a letter from the Higher Education Authority inviting the College to submit its views on the capital provisions which should be made on its behalf during the next decade and that these should be based on 'the allocation of disciplines laid down by the Government ... on July 6th'.

---

56 Pettit, op. cit.

57 McCartney, op. cit., Chapter 10, provides the most detailed published account of these events.

58 TCD Board Register, 13 November 1968. TCD archives, MUN/V/5/36.

59 Ibid. 22 January 1969.

60 TCD Board Register Companion Volume p. 23. TCD archives, MUN/V/6/14.

> The HEA also mentioned the need for consultation between University College and Trinity College down to departmental level ... especially in Medicine and Engineering. We wish to know whether University College would appoint members of the Medical and other appropriate departments to participate in discussions. Needless to say, if Engineering is to be the sole responsibility of University College, we anticipate that our staff will be invited to participate in formulating development proposals for Engineering at Belfield.[61]

This letter was approved by the Board at its meeting on 11 June 1969. The reply from the President was approved by the UCD Governing Body on 20 June. It read:

> Thank you for your letter of June 12th. As I think you know, this College considers the 'merger' plan of July 6th to be quite unworkable and does not accept the allocation of faculties therein laid down. It has gradually emerged from statements by members of the Government and from the attitude of the HEA that there will hardly be any forced imposition of that plan and allocation, if the principal aims of the Government can be otherwise achieved.
>
> At a recent meeting of representatives of the National University Senate with the HEA, it was pointed out by one of those representatives that economical collaboration ought properly to be arranged not merely between the two institutions in Dublin, but between the four in the Republic. ... The suggestion was welcomed by the entire meeting.[62]
>
> The National University Senate ... will have this matter before it on July 17th next. Meanwhile, our Governing Body has given approval to discussions between the four institutions if this should be agreeable.
>
> It is the view of our Governing Body that we cannot contemplate any changes in the faculties which are the integral parts of the College ... unless there is a clear prospect of a satisfactory future status for our own institution and of a good solution to the entire university question in the Republic. We are therefore submitting the estimates of future capital expenditure asked for by the HEA on the basis of all the existing activities of this College without either addition or subtraction.[63]

Despite the President's letter, Trinity did make its submission on capital requirements to the HEA in July 1969 'based on the assumption that Government policy in respect of the universities will be

---

61 Ibid.
62 The NUI Senate group met with the HEA on 27 May.
63 UCD Governing Body Minutes, 20 June 1969. UCD archives, GU2/29.

implemented.'⁶⁴ Nevertheless, it must have begun to feel that the political strategy of UCD in widening the merger debate by bringing in the colleges in Cork and Galway was bearing fruit. At the Board meeting of 25 June, there was an initial discussion about the possibility of collaboration between Trinity and the NUI.

The suggestion that Trinity might meet with representatives from the NUI obviously presented a serious dilemma to the Board. The Board had been relatively pleased with the prospect provided by the Lenihan plan and had co-operated with the HEA in discussions leading towards the implementation of that plan. On the other hand, there was considerable unease among a substantial number of academic staff in Trinity about the way things were progressing. This opposition ranged from conservative groups who deplored the acceptance of any interference with the identity of Trinity and the rights and privileges incorporated in its statutes, to a liberal group which saw the best way forward in the IFUT call for four co-operating universities and whose members had been practising that co-operation in the Council of IFUT. For the Board to reject a request from the NUI colleges in Dublin, Cork and Galway to discuss alternatives to the 6 July plan would have met with considerable hostility within the college.

By September when a formal invitation to meet with the NUI was issued to Trinity for 'exploratory discussions upon the possible ways of developing the future relationships between the two Colleges'⁶⁵ the Governing Body of UCD had already agreed to such a meeting.⁶⁶ The NUI invitation had suggested that the talks should be held with an independent chairman, a suggestion which the Provost rejected saying that 'an outside chairman would give the proceedings a formality and status to which the Board could not agree.' In his reply he continued:

> The Government has made decisions on the rationalisation and distribution of subjects between the two Colleges in Dublin and the Board has said quite publicly that it is prepared to accept these decisions, even though they involve considerable sacrifices from both Colleges. Reflection on the long series of meetings already held⁶⁷ between the Colleges on the

---

64 TCD Board Register Companion Volume. TCD archives, MUN/V/6/14 p. 83.
65 TCD Board Register, 24 September 1969, TCD archives, MUN/V/5/37.
66 See letter from Hogan to McConnell of 20 June quoted above.
67 His reference is obviously to the inconclusive meetings, under the chairmanship

question of subject distribution does not suggest that agreement would ever have been reached.... There can be no point in going over the same ground fifteen months after the Government announcement.⁶⁸

Eventually, however, the Provost did agree to meet, 'on a frank and informal basis,'⁶⁹ and the first meeting between the two sides took place on 7 January 1970.⁷⁰

Despite the obvious reluctance of Trinity to become involved in debates on alternative schemes, when meetings began in January, under the chairmanship of Dr Michael McCarthy, the President of UCC, progress was surprisingly swift. Although the Provost assured the Board meeting on 4 February that the distribution of subjects in the 6 July plan 'would continue to be the basis upon which our representatives would participate', by the time of its meeting on 6 March, the Board was informed that a document on the structure and functions of a Conference of Irish Universities had been agreed, that work was continuing on agreeing a document on the future government of the universities and that working parties had been established to consider the future of medical and engineering education.⁷¹

Even though the Board on 1 April was still asserting that its representatives should press for a distribution of subjects based upon the government's decision of 6 July, while accepting the principle of complementarity, by 8 April the Provost reported to the Board that an agreement had been reached which would be strongly recommended to the Senate of the NUI, to the Board of Trinity and to the Governing Body of UCD. The President of UCD reported similarly

of Dr Tarlach Ó Raifeartaigh, which took place between Trinity and UCD negotiation teams after the announcement of the O'Malley plan in April 1967.

68 UCD Governing Body Minutes, 25 November 1969, UCD archives, GU2/30. The Provost's letter is dated 24 October.

69 Ibid.

70 While agreeing to meet with the NUI, the Board did not give up its contacts with the HEA on the implementation of the 6 July plan. On 19 November, it agreed to forward to the Authority its proposals for 'a possible scheme of government of the future University of Dublin.' The letter from the Trinity Secretary which accompanied these proposals stated that the Board 'regards the acceptance of the July 6th distribution of subjects as an essential pre-requisite to the implementation of the decision to create a single University in Dublin.' TCD Board Register, 19 November 1969. TCD archives, MUN/V/5/37.

71 Ibid. 6 March 1970.

to the regular meeting of the Governing Body on 16 April and the agreement was debated at a special meeting on 23 April.[72]

The NUI/TCD agreement

The NUI/TCD agreement, as it quickly became known, set out a plan on the basis that there were to be four independent, co-operating universities in Ireland. In terms of the disposition of academic resources between the two Dublin universities it largely adhered to the subject distribution of the 6 July plan. The major change proposed was in relation to the key Faculty of Medicine. Lenihan had proposed that there be a single, unified, medical school and that it be located in Trinity. The agreement, however, proposed that pre-clinical medicine should remain in both universities with a conjoint board of the two universities established to manage a single clinical medical school located in three hospital centres. In return for this major concession by Trinity, it was to retain an engineering school concentrating on engineering science; Lenihan had proposed that engineering should be unified in UCD.[73] Law, veterinary medicine, and dentistry would go to Trinity, commerce, social science, agriculture and architecture to UCD, with arts and science in both.

The lengthiest part of the published agreement dealt with the future government of the universities and the control of the relationship between them. Appendix A of the agreement contained proposals for the constitution, functions and powers of the Conference of Irish Universities which had been proposed by the Commission and endorsed by Lenihan. It was to be an inter-university body with five elected representatives from each of the institutions and with significant powers including the power to appoint external examiners and to establish common minimum entrance standards for matriculated students. Appendix B set out a common structure for the government of the four new independent universities which drew on the traditional titles and practices of both Trinity and the NUI colleges.

---

72 The new-found accord between the Provost and the Presidents was illustrated when the Provost reported to the Board on 1 April that he had agreed to meet with the Presidents to develop, for the first time, a common approach to the government on academic salaries.

73 Engineering science, as envisaged in the agreement, was a theoretical study requiring no significant capital investment.

At the meeting of the Governing Body of UCD on 23 April the President commended the agreement to the members noting that, as the two Dublin colleges would have similar governing structures, he would now feel able to agree to transfer faculties from UCD to Trinity.[74] He laid particular emphasis on the proposed Conference of Irish Universities saying that it would, 'to some extent take the place of the National University. It would have less power in regard to individual institutions but it would give the universities a certain common ground and unity in relation to bodies such as the HEA.'[75] It was agreed to distribute copies of the agreement to the members of staff and, following meetings of the faculties and academic council, to meet again for a final consideration of the issue.

At a meeting of the Board in Trinity on the same day, it recorded its belief that 'the solution of the university question in Dublin presented to it was acceptable because it was the best that could be reached by agreement between the National University and Trinity College. It had special merit in that the reaching of this agreement had involved all the University Colleges and created the circumstances for future co-operation.'[76] As in UCD, it was agreed to take the views of the widest range of bodies in college before coming to a final decision.

Within Trinity there was broad approval for the agreement with some, not unexpected, reservations. The Medical Faculty regretted that the 6 July proposal for medicine was not being endorsed and the Business School was unhappy about its move to Belfield. On the other hand, the Engineering School was grateful for its reprieve. The Fellows and the non-Fellow professors were happy with the agreement and the ASA also endorsed it. When these views were reported to the Board it proceeded to confirm its acceptance of the agreement stating that:

> The agreed proposals on the future organisation of University Education in Ireland put forward by representatives of the university institutions, have created the circumstances necessary for future co-operation, are

---

74 The President had claimed earlier that, as the governing structures in Trinity were so different from those in the NUI colleges, it would be improper for him to agree to academic staff in areas such as veterinary medicine being consigned to Trinity.

75 UCD Minutes of Governing Body, 23 April 1970, UCD archives, GU2/30.

76 TCD Board Register, 23 April 1970, TCD archives, MUN/V/5/37.

the best that can be reached by agreement between them and the Board accepts them.⁷⁷

If there is a less than whole-hearted tone to this statement it surely arises from the feeling that the prize of the 6 July plan was no longer available to Trinity College.

The process of securing agreement in UCD was similar to that in Trinity although there were fewer regrets expressed. The President had felt sufficient confidence in the outcome that he had even referred the issue to the newly-formed staff-student committees,⁷⁸ which duly endorsed the agreement, as did all the faculties. The Academic Council approved the agreement by a vote of 47 to 1 with 5 abstentions. The ASA, which had been consulted for the first time by the college, expressed some reservations about the proposals for the structures of university government in the agreement but did not object to the proposed subject distribution.⁷⁹

In asking the Governing Body for its support the President emphasised that there was no certainty that the proposals would get a positive response from the HEA and from the government but he expressed his hope that they would be accepted. He stated that it was either the agreement or the 6 July plan. A vote was finally taken on a resolution which stated:

> The Governing Body accepts the proposals contained in [the NUI/TCD agreement], embodying the establishment of four independent and co-operating universities with broadly similar constitutions and the suggested distribution of faculties as between the two universities in Dublin.
>
> The Governing Body regrets the loss of the Faculties of Veterinary Medicine and Law.

The resolution was agreed *nem con*.⁸⁰

IFUT also welcomed the agreement. In a statement on 11 May 1970 it announced that 'The Council of IFUT welcomes and approves

77 Ibid., 9 May 1970, TCD archives, MUN/V/5/37.
78 The staff-student committees in UCD were established in 1968 in each faculty; they were seen as an attempt to forestall the student unrest which eventually did affect the college.
79 The ASA in UCD, from its inception, had as its major pre-occupation plans for the reform of the structures of university government. Its concern in this area was not mirrored in the ASA in Trinity.
80 UCD Governing Body Minutes, 5 May 1970, UCD archives, GU2/30.

the proposals which have been made for a mutually acceptable and academically suitable scheme of cooperation between the Irish Universities, as set out in the main document[81] of the T.C.D-N.U.I negotiations.'[82]

The Irish newspapers were occupied with other, more dramatic, issues at the time. On 5 May, they had announced the shock resignation of the Minister for Justice, Michael Moran and then, the following day, carried news of Jack Lynch's sacking from the cabinet of Charlie Haughey and Neil Blaney and the resignation of Kevin Boland. These cataclysmic political events were followed by the trial of Haughey and Blaney on the charge of attempting to import arms for use in the North. They immediately dwarfed any public interest in the merger of the Dublin colleges which was, in any event, beginning to lose its interest for people outside the academic world.

The NUI/TCD agreement was now with the HEA and the colleges waited for its judgement. As an added ingredient to the mix of considerations which the Authority had to weigh in coming to a decision, on 25 June, the Catholic hierarchy announced:

> Some hope of a change that would make [the] constitution [of Trinity College] acceptable to the Catholic conscience was provided by the announcement of a proposed merger—as it was called—of Trinity College and University College Dublin. This announcement enabled the bishops to reconsider the attitude that might be adopted to a new Trinity College. In consequence, the aptness of the existing statute has been examined on more than one occasion recently by the bishops.
>
> In view of the substantial agreement on basic issues that has been reached between the National University of Ireland and Trinity College, the hierarchy has decided to seek approval from the Holy See for the repeal of statute 287 of the plenary synod.[83]

After 95 years, the ban on the attendance of Catholics in Trinity College had finally been rescinded.

---

81 The main document referred to was the agreement on the allocation of faculties between the two Dublin colleges. Two appendices to the published agreement dealt with the government of the universities and the proposed Conference of Irish Universities; IFUT reserved judgement on these.
82 HEA papers for its meeting on 4 June 1970.
83 McCartney, op. cit.

7. The end of the affair

The HEA considers the agreement

The main focus of the HEA at this time was on the preparation of its recommendations on non-university, third level education in Dublin. The City of Dublin VEC had submitted a report to the Minister for Education in 1969 which proposed the establishment of a new Technological Higher Commercial College at Ballymun to accommodate most of the third-level courses carried out in its existing colleges in Bolton Street, Kevin Street and Rathmines. The Minister referred the VEC submission to the Authority which eventually, in December 1970, presented the Ballymun Report[1] to Minister Lenihan.

The HEA was also concerned at this stage with discussions concerning the legislation which would establish it on a statutory basis.[2] However, it was not unaware of the debate taking place between the NUI and TCD, having been alerted to the general progress of that debate by the academic members of the Authority. For example, at its meeting in January 1970, Ian Howie from Trinity advised the Authority that it would have to re-assess its position in regard to the merger and 'should take a positive attitude towards the present discussions between the NUI and TCD.' While Patrick Lynch from UCD stated that 'the Colleges would react very strongly against an imposed solution but ... would, at this stage, accept almost anything short of this.'[3]

---

1 *HEA Report on the Ballymun Project* (1972) Dublin, Stationery Office. Although the Authority agreed in large measure with the proposals from the VEC, a major row developed over the control of the proposed new institution, with the VEC objecting strongly to it being outside its own direct control. As a result, the report of the HEA was not published until 1972 and the National Institute for Higher Education, later to be Dublin city University, was eventually established in Ballymun completely independent of the VEC.
2 The Higher Education Authority Act was enacted in 1971.
3 HEA Minutes, 17 January 1970.

(Left) the Provost of Trinity, A. J. McConnell; (right) Michael Tierney, President of UCD in conversation (Irish Press)

In April 1970, a copy of the draft NUI/TCD agreement was submitted to the HEA which asked a working party to examine it. By October, 1970 the working party reported its initial conclusions that:

1) There was a substantial benefit to be gained from the fact that the two universities had come to an agreement.

2) There would be difficulties in the financial control of a joint Dublin university.

3) The HEA should accept the agreement on the allocation of faculties between the Dublin colleges.

4) The proposed Conference of Irish Universities should be established in legislation but the universities themselves should decide on the functions and powers allocated to it.

5) There should be one clinical medical school in Dublin.

No comment was offered by the working party on the basic premise of the agreement that there should be four, independent, universities rather than the three which would have emerged from the Lenihan and O'Malley plans.

Over the following months while the HEA considered its response to various aspects of the agreement, the universities made no preparations for the changes they had proposed in it. The one area where there was major concern was medical education. Letters were received by the Authority from a number of eminent medical practitioners pointing out the necessity to have just one large medical school in Dublin in order for it to reach an international level of resources in medical teaching and research.[4]

A draft final report from the working party was presented to the HEA in March 1971 and was generally accepted by it. This draft accepted the main provisions of the NUI/TCD agreement and, in particular, accepted the premise that there should be two co-operating universities in Dublin. The report was quickly completed and was presented to the Minister in December 1971 as the *Report on University Reorganisation*.[5] In this report, the HEA presented a comprehensive comparison of the virtues and defects of the Lenihan plan of July 1968 and the NUI/TCD agreement. On the key elements of the two plans it concluded as follows:

4 HEA Minutes, 5 January 1971.
5 HEA *Report on University Reorganisation* (1972) Dublin, Stationery Office.

One or two universities: There had been substantial change in the situation of Trinity College brought about by the removal of the ban on Catholic students attending there. Moreover, Trinity had undertaken to limit the number of non-Irish students to 10 per cent of the total and had already begun to implement this change. Furthermore, the fact that agreement had been reached in Trinity and UCD on the terms of the agreement indicated that, in the future, fruitful co-operation between the two colleges could be expected. It concluded that the factors which had precipitated the plans for a fusion of the two colleges no longer existed and it recommended that they should remain as separate institutions. However, it emphasised that 'there can never again be question of the two institutions pursuing an absolutely separate path'.[6]

Future co-ordination of the Dublin colleges: The Authority cast a fairly cold eye on the mechanisms proposed in the agreement to ensure that the promised transfers of faculties and other resources and the co-operation between the Dublin colleges actually took place. It did not believe that the proposed Conference of Irish Universities could achieve these ends. Instead, it recommended that the conjoint board proposed in the agreement to manage a combined clinical medical school should have its remit extended to cover the whole range of interactions between the colleges.

Medical education: The key issue of medical teaching was dealt with in a rather timid manner. The HEA stated:

> It is true that, in proposing only incomplete integration of Medical Teaching, the Agreement falls short of the ideal of a single school. We are convinced, however, that its plan for a joint Clinical School is the most that can be attained in the way of an agreed solution in this field. In view of the extremely complicated nature of the universities-cum-hospitals problems and the profoundly emotional issues involved in medical education, we believe that in a two Universities situation it would be unwise to press the matter further.[7]

The Authority, therefore, shied away from confronting the many influential interest groups involved in the arcane world of hospital and medical school politics and accepted the proposals in the agreement

---

6 Ibid., p. 59.
7 Ibid., p.60.

for separate pre-clinical schools and a joint clinical school managed by the conjoint board.

Engineering education: In approaching the topic of engineering education the Authority looked not just at the agreement but also at its recently published analysis of technological education in the Ballymun Report. It accepted the argument in the agreement that Trinity could retain a 'non-specialised course in Engineering Science'[8] as being complementary to the UCD school of engineering while keeping 'under constant review (1) the scale of University teaching of Engineering vis-à-vis that given in the Colleges of Technology'.

The Conference of Irish Universities: The Authority was not very enamoured with the proposals for a Conference of Irish Universities. It did not believe that the Conference as proposed would be an appropriate body to ensure co-operation and rationalisation between the separate university institutions and, particularly, between the two Dublin colleges. It saw the powers of the Authority itself as being necessary to achieve these goals. The Authority provided a lukewarm endorsement of the idea of a non-statutory conference which would be established on a voluntary basis by the universities themselves. And it saw any mandatory powers given to the Conference to be 'a serious encroachment on several principles of university autonomy.'[9] It concluded that the mission it saw for the conference was in 'the special and extremely important role ... as the constant upholder of that welcome spirit of co-operation between all our University institutions of which the first general manifestation [was] the NUI/TCD Agreement.'[10]

On all the other significant issues in the agreement, the HEA expressed its general support including the retention of Arts faculties in both colleges with physical sciences primarily in UCD and biological sciences primarily in Trinity. Unlike the agreement, the Authority did consider the situation of Maynooth in a new arrangement. However, just as in the report of the Commission on Higher Education, the

---

8 Some years later when the threat of a merger had finally receded, the Engineering School in Trinity reverted to the type of departmental organisation which is normal in engineering schools. Difficulties in securing accreditation from the professional engineering institutions, which required a specialised training built on a scientific foundation, may have contributed to this move.

9 HEA *Report on University Reorganisation* op. cit., p. 52.

10 Ibid., p. 55.

Catholic hierarchy was to be allowed to make its own decisions on what would be the best future arrangement for their college.

A new minister—a new plan

Following the publication of the *Report on University Reorganisation* by the HEA in 1972 it was generally assumed by the university authorities that there would be no further interference in their affairs by government. A general relaxation took place and no significant attempt was made by the university authorities to implement those changes which the agreement of 1970 had committed them to, apart from an enhanced cooperation between Trinity and the NUI colleges in areas such as salary negotiation. However, a change of government after a general election in 1973 brought a Fine Gael-led government into office and a new Minister for Education, Richard Burke. After 16 years in opposition the new government had many ideas which it was anxious to bring forward. Among these was a new plan for higher education.

The Burke plan, which was announced in December 1974, introduced some new elements to the debate of which the most significant, perhaps, was his reprieve for the NUI. The new NUI was to contain only two constituent colleges—UCC and UCG—but was to incorporate, as recognised colleges, the new National Institutes of Higher Education (NIHE)[11] in Dublin and Limerick. As far as Trinity and UCD were concerned, Burke accepted much of the HEA's recommendations but he gave UCD back its Law School and proposed that the Veterinary Medicine School should be based in UCD rather than in Trinity. Trinity would retain the unified Dental School and Pharmacy would be transferred from UCD to Trinity.

Although Trinity was unhappy about the Burke plan, it could be said that by this stage, politicians and public were suffering from merger fatigue; in fact, the most heated political debate on the Burke

---

11 The previous government's response to the persistent demand from interests in Limerick that a university should be established there was to create a new type of institution, a National Institute of Higher Education (NIHE), which, Brian Lenihan assured a Limerick audience, would be better than a university. The Limerick institute was joined by a similar institution in Dublin. Initially planned to resemble the German *fachhochshulen*, with an emphasis on science and technology, these NIHEs were later to become the University of Limerick and Dublin City University.

plan arose from its proposal that the NIHEs should be incorporated into the NUI. That proposal sparked a major dispute about whether the higher education system should be unitary or binary.

The NIHE group, led by Dr Edward Walsh, the Director of the NIHE in Limerick, argued strongly for the building up, in parallel with the university sector, of a non-university higher education sector incorporating the recently established Regional Technical Colleges (RTCs) with the NIHEs. The Minister, on the other hand, was proposing that the institutes should be incorporated into the university sector as recognised colleges of the NUI. The NUI meekly went along with the Minister's plans and, exercised its powers, for the first time in almost 70 years, to accept Limerick as a recognised college.[12] Limerick's tenure as a recognised college was not a happy one with recurring friction between the NUI and the NIHE. The uneasy relationship ended when the 1977 general election brought Fianna Fáil back to office and a new Minister, John Wilson, restored the *status quo ante*.

Burke's most significant legacies as Minister for Education were his decision to extend the period of primary teacher training to three years and to convince the universities that they should incorporate the teacher training colleges as recognised or associated colleges of the universities with access to primary degrees for their students. Richard Burke departed from office to become Ireland's European Commissioner in 1977 but before he left, two ideas in the merger plans were brought to fruition, although with contrasting outcomes.

A Conference of Irish Universities as a mechanism to bring the universities together, on a non-statutory basis, had been part of all the various plans put forward during the merger debates. Although the HEA had been lukewarm in its acceptance of the idea, it had been strongly championed by IFUT which saw it as an opportunity to introduce a more democratic ethos in the government of the university institutions. Accordingly, in 1973 Enda McDonagh, who was at that time a member of the Senate of the NUI as well as President of IFUT, pushed the Senate to take the initiative in setting up the Conference which it had presented as an integral part of the NUI/TCD agreement in 1970. It agreed to do this and with the co-operation of all the university institutions in Ireland, including Maynooth,

---

12 The National Institute in Dublin had not yet been formally established in 1974.

Queen's University Belfast and the New University of Ulster, an *ad hoc* Conference of Irish Universities (CIU) was established and had its first meeting in June 1974.[13]

The CIU was unusually egalitarian in its structure having five members from each institution comprising representatives of the governing bodies/board, the academic councils/senate, the general body of academic staff and the student body together with the president/provost *ex officio*. The President of UCC, Dr Michael D. McCarthy, was selected initially as the Chairman and Dr John Bourke, the Registrar of the NUI was appointed as its Executive Secretary. The first obstacle came when the HEA refused its request for funding, stating that it should be funded by the individual colleges from their annual block grants and indicating that it would not recommend that it be given statutory status. Nor was it very warmly welcomed by the college authorities despite the fact they had endorsed it as a key part of the NUI/TCD agreement. As early as January 1975, the Secretary of UCD, J. P. McHale, was writing to the governing body indicating his view that any powers given to the CIU would represent a dangerous intrusion on the autonomy of the college.

A parallel development, which probably explains the reluctance of the college authorities to support the CIU, was the development of a committee of the heads of the university colleges. This committee which later adopted the formal title, Committee of Heads of Irish Universities (CHIU),[14] was, as its name implies, confined to senior university administrators. It was thus able to avoid the complication of having input from academic staff and students in its discussions and submissions to government. IFUT warned from early on about the dangers of this development for the CIU and to no-one's surprise, when the *ad hoc* conference came back to its member institutions in 1975 for formal establishment, those same administrators were able to ensure that approval for its establishment was rejected. The CIU staggered on until 1979 when it adjourned *sine die*.[15] Its demise might

13 O'Flynn papers; to be deposited in UCD archives.

14 The committee was known initially as the Committee of Irish University Presidents and, in modern times, has transformed itself into the Irish University Association. It has always been a non-statutory body and is funded directly by the participating institutions.

15 The author chaired the final meeting of the Conference.

be seen as the last gasp of the democratic spirit which had invaded the university world in the 1960s.

The merger of the Schools of Dentistry and Veterinary Medicine

The rationalisation of teaching resources in Veterinary Medicine and Dentistry had been accepted by all parties as being desirable since the merger debates had begun. The road to a merger of these two faculties was somewhat unusual in that the funding of the agriculture and veterinary education sector came from the government Department of Agriculture rather than from Education. In 1976, the Minister for Agriculture, Mark Clinton, decided to effect the merger forthwith by cutting off the funding for the Trinity school and transferring it to the UCD school. A reasonably generous approach to staff in the Trinity school, allowing them to transfer to other science-based schools in Trinity and to maintain pension entitlements and membership of the Trinity Common Room, ensured that this element of the merger was accomplished with relatively little discord.[16]

A similar merger was carried through in the even more overlapping Dental Schools, without any heated debate—all the dental teaching moved to Trinity. At the same time, the School of Pharmacy, which was loosely attached to UCD, was also moved to Trinity.

The end of the great merger debate

The mergers of the Veterinary and Dentistry Faculties and the transfer of the School of Pharmacy, which involved the movement of about one hundred full-time students from UCD to Trinity and some 50 full-time students from Trinity to UCD, were the only tangible changes which resulted from a decade of heated debate among Dublin academics, many plans from three successive Ministers for Education and the HEA and from a great volume of contributions to the columns of the Dublin newspapers. Provision of resources to cope with a very large increase in the number of entrants to higher education was now of more concern to planners than satisfying the *amour propre* of the two Dublin university colleges. The number of new entrants to higher education in Ireland in 1964/5, as recorded by the Commission on Higher Education, was approximately 5,000. By

16 Coleman, op. cit., pp. 73–5.

1980 that number had jumped to 13,360 with a tenfold increase in the number of students attending in the technological sector.[17] The points race would soon replace the ban as a topic for editorial writers!

The NUI

No immediate change took place in the structures of the NUI. Dublin, Cork and Galway stayed shackled together with varying degrees of enthusiasm in the edifice that they had rejected. The teacher training colleges which were controlled by the Catholic authorities were accepted as recognised colleges of the NUI while their Church of Ireland counterpart, which had moved from Kildare Place to Rathmines in 1969, was taken under Trinity's wing. It was not until the passing of the 1997 Universities Act that significant alterations were made to the 1908 structures when the constituent colleges were given the novel status of constituent universities and Maynooth was finally given equal status with the other constituent bodies. The Act transferred most of the significant academic authority from the NUI to its constituent bodies, although their degrees continued to be awarded by the National University.

Trinity College

Trinity continued its move into the mainstream of Irish university education. It joined with the other universities in both the Conference of Irish Universities and the Committee of Irish University Heads and engaged in joint salary negotiations with the other colleges. It was, initially, a somewhat reluctant adherent to the Central Applications (CAO) system, being unhappy at relinquishing its relationships with its traditional feeder schools in favour of the purely objective criteria used by the CAO system. However, it did overcome its qualms eventually and joined in fully.

Trinity's commitment to reduce the number of non-Irish students attending was carried through. This move was associated with a small

17 The 1964/5 figures are extracted from Tables 9, 87 and 89 and from page 197 of the Commission's Report. The 1980 figures are from Table 1 in Patrick Clancy (1982) Participation in Higher Education Dublin, HEA. While the two sets of figures are not precisely comparable, they are broadly indicative of the trends over the period. The disproportionate increase in the number of entrants to the technological sector was centred in the ten new RTCs.

drop in the numbers of its students but at a time of rapidly increasing participation in higher education these numbers were soon restored.[18] It may be noted, also, that by the time of the first comprehensive survey of student participation in higher education in Ireland carried out by Patrick Clancy for the HEA in 1980,[19] there was little statistical difference between the origins of the student populations in Trinity and UCD. In that year, out of 1,182 new entrants to Trinity, 4.4 per cent were classified as foreign and 6.7 per cent were from Northern Ireland. For UCD in the same year out of 1,939 total new entrants, 2.3 per cent were classified as foreign and 2.3 per cent were from Northern Ireland.[20]

Maynooth

St Patrick's College, Maynooth remained a complex organisation. Governed as a single institution by the Catholic hierarchy, it had three separate identities—as a pontifical university, as a seminary and, in part, as a recognised college of the NUI. As was to be expected, given the deferential attitude at that time to the Church, the Commission on Higher Education in 1967 and the HEA in 1972 had refrained from making any specific directions about the future of Maynooth. However, in the expansive post-conciliar spirit prevailing in 1966, the bishops had announced the opening of the recognised college side of the institution to lay students.[21] Following this move, the number of full-time students in the recognised college increased from 477 in

---

18 HEA *Report on University Reorganisation*, op. cit., p. 117. The Report gives the numbers of full-time students in each of the university institutions in successive years. In Trinity, the numbers are listed as: 1968/69—3,913; 1969/70—4,005; 1970/71—3,915; 1971/2—3,867.

19 Clancy, op. cit.

20 Clancy's survey did not include any reference to the religious affiliation of entrants unlike the surveys of the Commission on Higher Education carried out two decades earlier. It did include data on the socio-economic status of new entrants; again the figures for Trinity and for UCD are very similar.

21 Matriculated clerical students at Maynooth spent their first three years studying for a BA or a BSc which was awarded by the NUI. They were taught by teachers who were recognised by the NUI as being suitably qualified and the courses were examined by UCD professors on behalf of the NUI. Funding for this element of Maynooth was provided by the state.

1968/9 to 852 in 1971/2[22] and the college became, for a time, an exciting centre for academic discourse and theological debate

The openness of the hierarchy to change was short-lived, however, as was shown a few years later when, in 1977, two lecturers, Malachi O'Rourke and P. J. McGrath, were dismissed from their positions, O'Rourke because of his recent laicisation and McGrath for 'writings prejudicial to church authority'. The dismissals were contested in the courts by the two academics, supported by IFUT. However, the Supreme Court upheld the dismissals and ruled that Maynooth was still essentially a seminary and, as such, properly governed by seminary discipline.[23] Its expansion continued but the conservative profile of the institution probably brought about the curious result that by 1980, when the Clancy survey was conducted on new entrants to Irish higher education institutions, Maynooth had a much higher proportion of females to males among its entrants than the other colleges and, despite its closeness to Dublin, it had a relatively small number of students from Dublin. Of its new entrants, Maynooth had 59.5 per cent female students compared to a a national figure of 47.7 per cent. Of that same cohort, only 19 per cent were from Dublin compared to 55 per cent in UCD and Trinity and 33 per cent nationally.[24]

Over the next decades Maynooth gradually assumed an academic profile similar to the other university colleges and in the 1997 Universities Act was finally granted equal status with the other colleges of the NUI with the rank of constituent university.

The National Institutes for Higher Education in Limerick and Dublin

As discussed above, the campaign to have a university institution based in Limerick had been carried on with varying degrees of intensity from the 1840s and with a renewed vigour by the Limerick University Project Committee, established in 1959. Although the proposal for

---

22 HEA *Report on University Reorganisation* p. 117. These figures represent an increase from 2.7 per to 4.3 per cent of the total number of students in university colleges in Ireland.

23. IFUT was pessimistic about the outcome of the case especially when, a short while before the delayed judgement was delivered, Chief Justice Tom O'Higgins was pictured in the daily newspapers leading a pilgrimage to Knock. The best narrative of these events is contained in Coleman, op. cit.

24 These figures are calculated from the data in Clancy, op. cit.

such a development had been rejected by the Commission on Higher Education and ignored by Donogh O'Malley in 1967, Brian Lenihan, in 1968, discussed with the HEA the idea of establishing a third-level technological institute in Limerick and of a council for educational awards which would award degrees in the institute. These two concepts eventually were realised as the National Institute for Higher Education in Limerick and the National Council for Educational Awards (NCEA). While the NIHE was looked upon with some suspicion by the project committee as being less than the university it sought, it was promoted by the Minister as the flagship institution in a technological stream of higher education which would include the RTCs and which would run alongside the traditional university stream in a binary system.

Dr Edward Walsh was appointed as Director of the NIHE in 1969 and proceeded with great vigour to develop the new institution, proclaiming its technological spirit and attacking the liberal ethos of the existing 'old' universities. This campaigning approach led to a stark conflict when Minister Richard Burke, in his 1974 plan, decided that the NIHE should become a recognised college of the NUI and have its degrees awarded by the NUI rather than by the NCEA. Walsh led a vigorous campaign against this development and, at one stage, inspired his students to refuse to accept the NUI degrees. Burke's stormy period as Minister ended with his transfer to Brussels in 1976. His policy for the NIHE was reversed on the defeat of the coalition government in 1977. The new Fianna Fáil Minister, John Wilson, restored the binary divide between the university and the technological sectors, the NUI breathed a sigh of relief at having its unwilling and unruly associate removed from its care and the NCEA welcomed back its degree-awarding faculties.

Meanwhile, back in Dublin, the Burke plan in 1974 had proposed the establishment of a second NIHE for the Dublin area and the Minister appointed a governing body for the new institution in June 1975. Patrick Donegan, the Chair of the City of Dublin Vocational Education Committee (CDVEC) was appointed to chair the governing body and Dr Danny O'Hare was appointed as Director of the still notional institute in October 1976. Whereas to many people the logical plan appeared to be that the NIHE would start with a transfer of the existing third-level courses which had been run by the CDVEC in Bolton Street, Kevin Street and Rathmines to the new institution, the CDVEC did not welcome the removal of the jewels in its crown. There followed a long period of argument and conflict between the CDVEC and a succession of ministers for education about the way forward. This resulted eventually in the establishment of the Dublin Institute of Technology by the CDVEC from its existing institutions—without any transfer of courses or staff—and the start-up of the NIHE in 1980 with a completely new cohort of staff and students on the site of the Albert Agricultural College in North Dublin, which had been vacated by UCD in its move to Belfield.

The two NIHEs developed along similar paths with the Dublin college specialising in the biological sciences while Limerick emphasised its engineering character. They both received statutory recognition in 1980 and eventually achieved university status through legislation in 1989, becoming Dublin City University and the University of Limerick.

The Irish Federation of University Teachers

IFUT, which had been founded in 1963, retained a strong interest in professional concerns. Inflationary trends in the 1970s created great pressure on it to become involved in salary negotiation and to become a trade union. After considerable internal debate, it sought and obtained trade union status in 1976 and affiliated to the Irish Congress of Trade Unions in 1979. Its most significant involvement in professional affairs in later years was its very active role in the discussions prior to the enactment of the Universities Act in 1997. The inclusion in the Act of an important definition of academic freedom and of a substantial involvement by students and non-professorial staff in the governance of the universities might be seen as a final victory for the spirit of the *soixante-huitards* of Paris, 29 years later.

The Higher Education Authority

In addition to its advisory role, the HEA was set up to act as a semi-independent buffer between the universities and the Department in the financing of university education. This function was to continue and develop although the independence of the Authority from the

Department became less clear in later years. Statutorily independent, any danger that the HEA might become overly autonomous in its thinking was counteracted by the fact that the position of Chairman was invariably filled by retired Secretaries or Secretaries-general of the Department of Education. The fact that the current Chair of the Authority is from the world of business without any prior experience in educational administration is evidence of a new way of thinking about education in the corridors of power rather than a new way of thinking about the appropriate level of independence of such bodies as the HEA.

Initially the funding remit of the HEA was confined to the five university institutions of 1968. Today it has responsibility for seven universities, 13 Institutes of Technology and seven designated institutions including the Colleges of Education, the National College of Art and Design and the Royal Irish Academy. Reflecting this change, only 26 per cent of the members of the Authority are university academics compared to 47 per cent of the first authority in 1968.

Conference of Heads of Irish Universities/Irish Universities Association

As discussed above, the brief life of the Conference of Irish Universities was effectively terminated by the rise of regular meetings of the five university heads in an informal group called, initially, the Committee of Heads of Irish Universities. This body later changed its title to the Conference of Heads of Irish Universities (CHIU) and expanded its membership to seven with the designation as universities of the University of Limerick and Dublin City University in 1989. It was incorporated as a company in 1997 and eventually became the Irish Universities Association in 2005. It is now accepted by government, if not by the academic staff of the universities, as the official voice of the university sector.

Regional Technical Colleges/Institutes of Technology

The idea of Regional Technical Colleges (RTCs) was first put forward by Minister Patrick Hillery in 1963. Originally intended to be, primarily, second level colleges, their mission was changed when it became clear that there was a significant shortage of technician training places in Ireland. The first three RTCs opened in 1970 and their numbers grew over the years so that today there are 14 colleges spread throughout the country. Although some of the colleges, such as that in Cork, were formed from amalgamation of existing further and higher education institutions, most of them were entirely new institutions with new, young academic staff.

The colleges originally concentrated on two-year certificate or three-year diploma courses; in the late 1970s they began to teach to primary degree level and later to master and doctorate level. Their curricula concentrated on engineering, science and business; their awards were granted by the NCEA which was established in 1972 and put on a statutory basis in 1979. In the late 1990s, pressure came from the colleges to rename them in order to reflect their increased level of responsibility and they were designated as Institutes of Technology (IT). The NCEA was split into the Higher Education and Training Council (HETAC) and the Further Education and Training Council (FETAC) and the ITs were given delegated authority to make most of their awards autonomously. In 2006 the institutes were transferred from the supervision of the Department to the care of the HEA.

Dublin Institute of Technology

Developments in the non-university, higher education sector in Dublin over this period provide a most intriguing political and educational picture.[25] By the early 1970s, the City of Dublin Vocational Education Committee (CDVEC) under the redoubtable chairmanship of Patrick Donegan had under its wing an array of colleges offering a wide range of second and third level education. At third level, these colleges included such long-established and reputable institutions as Bolton Street and Kevin Street, specialising in science, engineering and architecture, the College of Commerce in Rathmines, the Dublin College of Music in Chatham Street and the college in Cathal Brugha Street, devoted to catering and food technology. Their awards were validated autonomously and by various outside professional bodies.

As discussed earlier, one of the HEA's first tasks when it was established in 1968 was to develop proposals for a new third level college in Dublin at Ballymun which would include most of the advanced third level resources from the CDVEC but would be independent from

25 This is well chronicled by White op. cit.

it in its management and control.[26] That 'takeover bid' was strongly resisted by the CDVEC which also resisted moves by government to have its course validation carried out by the newly established NCEA. Instead, it formed an alliance with Trinity College in 1975 whereby Trinity would provide validation for its degree courses.[27] This proved to be somewhat of a pyrrhic victory as, when the new college in Dublin was established in Ballymun as the National Institute for Higher Education in Dublin, later to become Dublin City University, it was completely independent of the CDVEC and its awards were validated by the NCEA.

In 1978, the CDVEC made an order establishing the Dublin Institute of Technology (DIT), which was to incorporate all its higher education facilities under a single governing body. Since then the DIT has successfully established its identity in the public mind and has campaigned for its re-location on a single new site and for its designation as a university. These objectives have been partly realised by the announcement in July 2012 that funding for the development of a new DIT campus at Grangegorman will shortly be available.

Here we go again

In March 2009 Trinity and UCD announced the establishment of a formal merger of research activities in an Innovation Alliance.

In January, 2010, the Minister for Education, Batt O'Keefe, announced plans to abolish the NUI.

In 2011 it was reported that a complete merger of UCD and Trinity was being considered by advisers to the government. The following year a report commissioned by the HEA from 'international experts' recommended the merger of UCD and Trinity.

---

26 HEA *Report on the Ballymun Project*, op. cit.
27 Undoubtedly, Trinity viewed this alliance as giving it reinforcement in its resistance to elements of the unwelcome Richard Burke plan of 1974.

A QUESTION OF IDENTITY

Appendix 1. *Taoisigh and Ministers for Education 1959–87*

Taoisigh

Seán Lemass 1959–66

Jack Lynch 1966–73

Liam Cosgrave 1973–7

Jack Lynch 1977–9

Charles Haughey 1979–81

Garret FitzGerald 1981–2

Charles Haughey 1982

Garret FitzGerald 1982–7

Ministers for Education

Patrick Hillery 1959–65
George Colley 1965–66

Donogh O'Malley 1966–68
Brian Lenihan 1968–69
Padraig Faulkner 1969–73

Richard Burke 1973–6
Peter Barry 1976–7

John Wilson 1977–79

John Wilson 1979–81

John Boland 1981–2

Martin O'Donoghue 1982

Gemma Hussey 1982–6
Patrick Cooney 1986–7

Appendix 2. *Membership of Commission on Higher Education, appointed November 1960; reported February 1967*

Chairman: An Príomh Bhreitheamh Cearbhall Ó Dálaigh

Dr C. S. Andrews, Chairman, Córas Iompar Éireann
Daniel Buckley, B.A., Secondary teacher
Professor Herbert Butterfield, D. Litt., Master of Peterhouse, Cambridge
Sean Ó Cadhla, M.A., former Chief Inspector of National Schools
Professor Charles F. Carter, M.A., Professor of Political Economy, University of Manchester
Phillis Bean Uí Ceallaigh, M.Sc.
Máirín Bean Uí Chinnéide, M.A.
Most Reverend William Conway, D.D., D.C.L. *(resigned on being appointed Archbishop of Armagh in 1964)*
Lieutenant General Michael J. Costello, General Manager, Comhlucht Siúicre Éireann, Teo.
Martin Cranley, M.Sc., Principal, College of Science and Technology, Kevin Street, Dublin
John Dempsey, B.Sc., A.R.C.Sc.I., former Secretary, Department of Agriculture
An Bráthair S. de Faoite, B.A., Árd-Mháistir, Scoil na mBráthar, Sráid Sheasnáin, Luimneach
Labhrás Ó Gotharaigh, B.Agr.Sc., Headmaster, Vocational School, Portumna, Co. Galway
Dr Juan Greene, former President, National Farmers' Association
Joseph Griffin, Director, Irish Glass Bottle Co. Ltd
Seán Ó Lideadha, National Teacher
Liam Ó Luanaigh, Cathaoirleach, Comhdáil Náisiúnta na Gaeilge
Professor Edward Keenan, Dean, Faculty of Medicine, University College, Dublin *(replaced on his death in 1962 by Professor Eoin O'Malley)*
Dr James J. McElligot, former Governor, Central Bank of Ireland and former Secretary of the Department of Finance

Professor John J. McHenry, M.A., D.Sc., F.Inst.P., Professor of Experimental Physics, University College, Cork

Very Reverend Patrick J. McLaughlin, B.D., D.Sc., P.P., former Professor of Experimental Physics, St Patrick's College, Maynooth

Professor James Mitchell, B.Sc., B.E., F.G.S, Registrar, University College, Galway

Professor Theodore W. Moody, M.A. Ph.D., D.Litt., F.T.C.D., Professor of Modern History, Trinity College, Dublin

Patrick G. Murphy, B.Sc., M.E., M.I.E.E., M.I.Mech.E. Chief Engineer, Electricity Supply Board

The Right Reverend Richard Gordon Perdue, D.D., Bishop of Cork, Cloyne and Ross

The Most Reverend William Philbin, Bishop of Clonfert

Dr Thomas Walsh, Director, An Foras Talúntais

Secretary: Séamus Ó Cathail
Assistant Secretary: Liam Ó Fearghaill

Appendix 3. *Membership of first Higher Education Authority, appointed 16 August 1968*

Chairman : Tarlach Ó Raifeartaigh, Chairman of the Committee for Higher Education & Research, Council of Europe

Donal O'Carroll, Chairman & Chief Executive of P. J. Carroll & Co.

Tadhg Ó Ciardha, Registrar and Professor of Statistics, University College, Cork

Máirín Bean Uí Chinnéide, writer

Hugh de Lacy, Principal, Kevin Street College of Technology

John Garvin, Chairman of An Comhairle Leabharlanna

John Grainger, Professor of Zoology & Comparative Anatomy, Trinity College, Dublin

Ian Howie, Registrar and Associate Professor of Zoology, Trinity College, Dublin

Patrick Lynch, Associate Professor of Applied Economics, University College, Dublin

Martin McCourt, Managing Director, General Electric Co., Ireland

Eoin McCarthy, Chairman, Technical Information Division, Institute of Industrial Research & Standards

Thomas Murphy, Registrar and Professor of Social & Preventive Medicine, University College, Dublin

Jeremiah Newman, President, St Patrick's College, Maynooth

Colm Ó hEocha, Professor of Biochemistry, University College Galway, and Chairman of the National Science Council

Brendan Senior, Agricultural and Business interests

Secretary: James F. Dukes

Appendix 4. *Provosts/Presidents of Irish university institutions 1908–80*

Trinity College, Dublin
  Anthony Trail 1904–14
  John Pentland Mahaffy 1914–19
  John Henry Bernard 1919–27
  Edward John Gwynn 1927–37
  William Edward Thrift 1937–42
  Ernest Henry Alton 1942–52
  Albert Joseph McConnell 1952–74
  F. S. L. Lyons 1974–81

University College, Cork
  Sir Bertram Windle 1904–19
  Patrick Merriman 1919–43
  Alfred O'Rahilly 1943–54
  Henry St John Atkins 1954–63
  John J. McHenry 1964–67
  Michael D. McCarthy 1967–78

University College, Dublin
  Denis J. Coffey 1908–40
  Arthur Conway 1940–47
  Michael Tierney 1947–64
  Jeremiah Hogan 1964–72
  Thomas Murphy 1972–85

University College, Galway
  Alexander Anderson 1899–1934
  Mgr John Hynes 1934–45
  Mgr Pádraig de Brún 1945–59
  Martin Newell 1960–75

Bibliography

MANUSCRIPT MATERIAL

Higher Education Authority archives
Minute books of HEA meetings

Irish Federation of University Teachers archives
Minute books and papers of the Council of the Irish Federation of University Teachers

National Library of Ireland
Sheehy Skeffington Collection

National University of Ireland archives
Minute books of Senate of the National University of Ireland

National University of Ireland Galway archives
Minute books of Governing Body of University College Galway

Trinity College Dublin Library, Manuscripts Department
Board Registers: MUN/V/5/12–42
Interviews with Prof. George Dawson: TCD Tape 161–164 9932/84

University College Cork archives
Minute books of Governing Body of University College Cork

University College Dublin archives
Academic Staff Association papers
R. D. Edwards papers: LA22/203, 206, 219, 239, 244
Governing Body papers: GV2/33, 34
Roger McHugh papers
James Meenan papers
Michael Tierney papers
Patrick J. O'Flynn papers (relating to the Conference of Irish Universities and the Irish Federation of University Teachers) to be deposited.

BIBLIOGRAPHY

UK PARLIAMENTARY PAPERS

Report of Committee
Higher Education—Report of the Committee appointed by the Prime Minister under the Chairmanship of Lord Robbins 1961–63 London, HMSO (1963)

UK Legislation
Maynooth College Establishment Act 1795
An act to enable her majesty to endow new colleges for the advancement of learning in Ireland 1845
Irish Universities Act, 1908. 8 Edw. VII(1908)

IRISH PARLIAMENTARY PAPERS

Irish Government Reports
Investment in Education [Prl 8311] (Dublin 1965)
Science and Irish Economic Development (1965)
Commission on Higher Education 1960–1967: I Presentation and Summary of Report [Prl 9326] (Dublin, 1967)
Commission on Higher Education 1960–1967: II Report Vols. 1 and 2 [Prl 9389] (Dublin, 1967)
Higher Education Authority: Report on University Reorganisation [Prl 2276] (1972)
Higher Education Authority: Report on the Ballymun Project (1972)
Report of Commission on accommodation needs of the constituent colleges of the National University of Ireland [Pr 5089](1959)
Report of the Board of Visitors to University College, Dublin (1960)
Dáil Éireann debates
Seanad Éireann debates

Irish Legislation
University Education (Agriculture & Dairy Science) Act 1926 [No 32 of 1926]
University College Galway Act, 1929 [No 35 of 1929]
University College Dublin Act, 1960 [No 16 of 1960]
Higher Education Authority Act, 1971 [No 22 of 1971]
University of Limerick Act, 1989 [No 14 of 1989]
Universities Act, 1997 [No 24 of 1997]
The Trinity College, Dublin (Charters and Letters Patent Amendment) Act, 2000.

CONTEMPORARY NEWSPAPERS, PERIODICALS, JOURNALS AND REPORTS

The Irish Times, 1960–74
Irish Independent, 1960–74
Irish Press, 1960–74
Contemporary Developments in University Education (1963, 1964, 1965, 1966, 1967, 1971) Reports on seminars held by the Academic Staff Association of UCD
Tuairim (1960) *UCD and the Future*
University College Dublin and the Future (1960) Memorandum from a research group of Tuairim, Dublin branch
University Education in Ireland (1974) Report on seminar held by the Irish Federation of University Teachers
University entrance requirements and their effect on second level curricula (1979) Proceedings of a seminar organised by the Irish Federation of University Teachers

SECONDARY SOURCES

Books
Aldous, Richard (2006) *The Lion and the Unicorn—Gladstone vs Disraeli* London, Hutchinson
Balfour, Sebastian, L. Howes, M. De Larrabeiti, A. Weale (Eds.) (2009) *Trinity Tales—Trinity College Dublin in the Sixties* Dublin, The Lilliput Press
Brady, Conor (2005) *Up with the Times* Dublin, Gill & Macmillan
Brown, Terence (2004) *Ireland: A social and cultural history 1922–2002* London, Harper Perennial
Callanan, Frank (Ed.) (2005) *The Literary & Historical Society 1955–2005* Dublin, A. and A. Farmar
Clancy, Patrick (1982) *Participation in Higher Education: A National Survey* Dublin, Higher Education Authority
Coleman, Marie (2000) *IFUT—A History* Dublin, Irish Federation of University Teachers
Coolahan, John (1981) *Irish Education—History and Structure* Dublin, Institute of Public Administration
Corcoran, T. (Ed.) (1932) *Ollsgoil na h-Éireann: The National University handbook 1908–1932* Dublin, Sign of the Three Candles